NO MORE
ORDINARY
living *the life you were* made *for*

by
CAROL BURTON McLEOD

Bridge-Logos

Alachua, Florida 32615

Endorsements

Carol McLeod and I have been friends since college days and I am thrilled to observe how God is using her at this moment in history. Carol's new book, *No More Ordinary* is just what you have been looking for in order to live the life of God's dreams for you. Regardless of your circumstances or your failures, God has an extraordinary life for you! The principles for living that you will discover between the pages of Carol book will empower you, excite you and challenge you.

Lisa Osteen Comes—Associate Pastor at Lakewood Church in Houston, TX and author of *You Were Made for More!*

I'm convinced that most people fail because they don't understand the importance of priorities. Carol McLeod understands the power of what's important in life and her new book *No More Ordinary: Living the Life You Were Made For!* will change the way you think about the future. If you want to accomplish something significant, your first step is to read this book. It's time to change things. Read it, and start.

Phil Cooke, Ph.D.—Filmmaker, Media Consultant, and Author of *One Big Thing: Discovering What You Were Born to Do*

Life can be really hard and is often filled with questions that go unanswered and situations that just don't make sense. It can cause us to wonder where God is and is He really FOR us. In this book, Carol masterfully weaves together promises from God's Word with stories of men and women who dared to believe God even when faced with unimaginable circumstances. Carol reminds us that God is always faithful and trustworthy. Whether our dark pit is caused by choices other people made toward us, or poor choices we made ourselves, God brings the dead back to life. It's never too late for us to have an abundant life in Christ!

Holly Moore—Vice President of Growing Leaders

Carol "gets it" when it comes to the meaning of life! If you have wondered how to tap into the promise of abundant life, this book, "No More Ordinary" has all the secrets ... which have never really been secrets at all. Her writing style is hopeful, joyful, and firmly tethered to the truth found in the Bible. Finally, Carol has written a book to BOTH men and women! Carol tells a story like no one else can ... wrings the truth out of "passage" of Scripture ... and clearly presents a challenge to live the life that you were made for!"

Lynette Troyer Lewis—Author of *Climbing the Ladder in Stilettos*, featured in The Wall Street Journal, The New York Post, The Dallas Morning News, and on The Today Show

We all want to have a life that's richly satisfying and significant. But many times, in the midst of its ups and downs, we end up settling for less than God's best. We allow discouragement to distract us from the joy to be found in every day.

In her new book, Carol encourages us to keep our focus on the hope today holds. Her passion for living life with gusto will inspire you to do the same. The stories and truths she shares will motivate you to find God's best for your life, and to live it with passion every single day.

Jim and Tamara Osteen Graff—Pastors, Faith Family Church in Victoria, TX, author of best selling book, *A Significant Life,* and Founders of The Significant Church Network

Reading *No More Ordinary* will help you see that when you get connected with your Creator, you will discover the gifts He has placed within you, which He wants to use to have an impact upon others. He never intended for you or anyone just to exist. Even difficult experiences can be turned around by God and can be used to help others.

Carol shares that when you seek to hear and obey God, He will give you supernatural insight and favor and work miraculously in and through your life.

Sharon Daugherty—Senior Pastor
Victory Christian Center, Tulsa, Oklahoma

Are you longing for more in your spiritual journey? Read this book. With passion and purpose, Carol invites us into the adventure of abundant life in Christ. You'll be inspired and uplifted along the way.

Becky Harling—International speaker and author of *The 30 Day Praise Challenge, Rewriting Your Emotional Script, Freedom From Performing,* and *Finding Calm in Life's Chaos*

What's not to love about Carol McLeod? She is a dynamic leader, outstanding speaker, and a true woman of God. Her new book *No More Ordinary* is another outstanding expression of God's abundant, extraordinary, extravagant life that for most Christians seems just outside their grasp. Carol's latest writing helps people go beyond being too easily pleased and to step into God's fullest expression of life, in a most practical way.

Paul said it like this, "So here I am writing and preaching about things that are way over my head, the inexhaustible riches and generosity of Christ. My task is to bring out in the open and make plain what God, who created all of this in the first place, has been doing in secret and behind the scenes all along. Through followers of Jesus like yourselves gathered in churches, this extraordinary plan of God is becoming known and talked about even among the angels!" (Ephesians 3:8-10, MSG). Why is this important? It is because the Bible is about ordinary people doing extraordinary things (See Acts 4:13).

God's plan for you is the extraordinary! This word means: surpassing the norm; to break status quo (accepting things as they are); to exceed common, usual, or mundane; it is life that is exceptional, remarkable, amazing, unimaginable ... well, abundant! This is what Carol's book unfolds to you in a remarkable way!

Ron McIntosh—President, Ron McIntosh Ministries and I.M.P.A.C.T., author of four books, including the best-selling, *The Greatest Secret*

You're an original. There's no one like you, and never will be. So what's God's unique plan for you? *No More Ordinary* is a fresh word on what Jesus really said about abundant living and living the life God dreams for you. The teaching and amazing stories uncover how famous and not so famous people lived a life so abundant that (as Carol says) "heaven stood to its feet and cheered!" You will finish this book determined to live well, full of hope and expectation. I promise.

John Mason, Author of *An Enemy Called Average* and many other bestselling books

"When I was a child,..." If you are ready to shun ordinary living for the grown-up version of abundance, this latest by Carol McLeod is your guide. Most of us have been guilty of cheapening faith, of lowering the standards of a good life to the best of what we have observed in this world. But, none of that. Herein lives some really good news. We've aimed too low. And yes, God has prepared something far better for us. So settle in and get ready to unveil the highest arc for your life—the trajectory of the life you were made for.

Chris Busch—Founder and CEO of Lightquest Media

Carol McLeod's newest book, *No More Ordinary,* leads Christians into a more intimate walk with their Creator. Not just because it's the right thing to do, but because HE IS WORTHY of our ALL—all our time, all our effort, all our dreams. This book is loaded with story after story of God's faithfulness to His servants— inspiring readers to continue in our pursuit of Him, His Word even in the face of hardship. This book could have only been written by someone who has first been with the Savior. I believe Carol has and this book is evidence of that!

Johnie Hampton—President & CEO of Hampton Creative in Tulsa, OK

Bridge-Logos

Alachua, FL 32615 USA

No More Ordinary

Carol Burton McLeod

Unless otherwise indicated, the Scripture quotations in this
publication are from the Revised Standard Version (RSV) of
the Bible.

All Greek references are from *Sparkling Gems from the Greek,*
Rick Renner.

Printed in the United States of America.

Library of Congress Catalog Card Number: 2013955938
International Standard Book Number 978-1-61036-120-0

VP 01-09-14

Contents

Endorsements ii

Dedications viii

Introduction 1

Much More! 5

A Bigger Shovel 19

The Greatest Love Story Ever Told 29

The Gut-wrenching Discipline of Abundant Living 49

Reality Bible 61

The Thrill of a Defiant Life! 83

Gifts That Trump Human Pain 103

Abundant, Lavish, and More! 127

Choose Life ... Choose Well! 147

A Life of Miraculous Intervention 167

Living for Legacy 187

Acknowledgements 205

Dedications

Lovingly dedicated to My Three Sons Matthew, Christopher and Jordan

Matthew ... My first born ...

You have led the way for the rest ... and what an excellent example and caring leader you have always been!

I have always loved being your mom ... and now I love being your friend! You have always exhibited a passion and focus that is uncommon in this common world.

Thank you for adding Emily, Olivia, Wesley and Boyce to the family McLeod!

Most of all, thank you for loving God, for making an impact in His Kingdom and for living an extraordinary life.

Christopher ... The one who came next ...

You arrived with a song in your heart and a sparkle in your eyes.

Thank you for being patient with a technologically impaired mother and for lending your excellence and expertise to every conversation.

Thank you for dreaming big dreams.

Thank you for adding Liz and Amelia to our family.

Most of all, thank you for serving God, for your love of worship and for rising above the ordinary.

Jordan ... The miracle boy ...

You came after years of infertility and disappointment ... and my life has never been the same. You are the tangible evidence that God answers prayers.

Thank you for phone calls during Duke games and Buffalo Bills games and for loving Christmas as much as I do!

Thank you for the gifts of Allie and Ian.

Most of all, thank you for your heart of compassion, your joy of living and for refusing to live an ordinary life.

Introduction

IT is true, you know. God unquestionably has a magnificent plan for your life beyond anything you could ever dream or imagine. Jesus absolutely came to Earth for more than just dealing with your sin issues ... He came to leave a deposit of Heaven's extravagance in your daily existence.

I don't know what kind of life you are living today, but I can guarantee there is more life at your disposal than you have ever dreamed of, asked for, or imagined. God never meant for His children to live a mediocre, gray existence of daily exasperation and frustration. God, who is no small-thinking God, has a life for you that reeks of Heaven's glory and is lavishly splattered with the joy of His presence.

> If you are dealing with the pain of your circumstances today ... then this book is for you.
>
> If you are dealing with the shame of past choices and unfair events ... then this book is for you.
>
> If you are wondering why you are here at this moment in history ... then this book is for you.
>
> If you are determined not to waste one minute ... not one hour ... not one day of this incredible life that you have been given ... then this book is for you.
>
> If you long to wring the joy out of the miracle that is an ordinary day ... then this book is for you.

Tackling Life

No More Ordinary tackles the issue of abundant life at its very core. It smashes the false suppositions that abundant life can be measured in pay raises and bonuses or weighed by trips to Disney World, Hawaii, and the spa. This book may also convince you that the equation for abundant life does not necessarily include gorgeous, healthy spouses, or even 2.8 well-behaved and brilliant children. The life for which Jesus died may not even include Harvard, a colossal Christmas every year, or the house of your dreams. If tangible items and mere creature comforts are your expectant thoughts when you imagine "abundance" ... may I just say you have set your expectations way, way too low?

> "If we consider the unblushing promises of reward and the staggering nature of the rewards promised in the Gospels, it seems that our Lord finds our desires not too strong, but too weak. We are half-hearted creatures, fooling about with drink and sex and ambition when infinite joy is offered us, like an ignorant child who wants to go on making mud pies in a slum because he cannot imagine what is meant by the offer of a holiday at the sea. We are far too easily pleased." — C.S. Lewis

No More Ordinary digs deeply into the Word of God and presents answers concerning the definition and the purpose of living the life of God's dreams for you. I happen to believe the Bible is a dependable GPS for all of life's deepest questions and has the final answer on everything to do with life.

Heroes and Heroines

Each chapter tells in two parts the story of a man or woman who defied their circumstances and lived a life so abundant that Heaven stood to its feet and cheered! The life story of these heroes and heroines of the faith begin each chapter, but you will not learn the "rest of their story" until the concluding sentences of the chapter. Some of these life stories will be about people whose legacy is well known and their names will be familiar to you. However, some of the life stories are about men and women whose names will never be written in any history book other than God's.

The final chapter, "Living for Legacy," does not present a challenging biography until the very end of the chapter, which is also the end of the book.

Practical Application

At the conclusion of each chapter you will find several other helpful and life-enhancing components.

The closing prayer at the end of each chapter is one I hope you will pray out loud in order to sear the truth of that specific chapter into your life. Part of our ability to access the life God has for us happens when we pray. God never ignores one of His children who come to Him in sincere and heartfelt prayer.

The declaration at the end of the chapter is intended for you to say out loud. Our tongues are a creative force from which we have not yet begun to realize or utilize their power. When you declare the promises of God out loud, hell shakes and Heaven applauds!

You will also find a verse of Scripture at the close of each chapter. My prayer is that you will commit this Scripture to memory and allow it to become part of who you are. The life God has for us can never be accessed, experienced, or known without time spent in the Word of God. Trust me ... I know!

And finally, there is a quote at the end of every chapter. Sometimes this quote is from the person whose life is chronicled in the chapter, other times the quote matches the chapter in theme. My prayer is that these particular quotes, spoken by those who have gone before and tapped into the depth of abundant life, will challenge you to live life at full-throttle ... holding nothing back!

At First and Finally

And finally, my deepest hope and prayer is that, after reading this book, your determination will change. I pray you will determine to live well ... to live with hope and expectation. I hope you will resolve to leave behind the grayness of a black and white existence and tap into the glory and grandeur of friendship with God. My desire is that this book will propel you into tackling life with gusto and with the thrill of possibility. I am praying the chains of shame, regret, and discouragement that have held you back will disappear as you understand the power of living wholeheartedly and passionately.

Every one of us must accept responsibility for our own lives with no blame or aspersions cast in the direction of others and their choices. You, in partnership with God, will design the life that will occupy the length of your days. While you may not be able to determine all of the events and circumstances of your life, the atmosphere of your life is entirely up to you. You create your life with every prayer you choose to pray, every word you choose to speak, every person whom you choose to emulate, and every mountain you choose to conquer. I pray you will learn, before it is too late, to live before you die.

Life with gusto! Live with joy! There will be days when you will have to remind yourself to just keep breathing ... but those days will pale in comparison to the days that take your breath away! It is time to choose the life of God's dreams for you every waking hour of every glorious day.

CHAPTER 1

Much More!

LIFE! You have been given life by the One who is known as Life himself. What an extraordinary and miraculous way to describe oneself, *"I am the Way ... the Truth ... and the Life!"* All other attempts at living begin and end with the One who threw the rainbows into the stormy sky, who placed the brilliance into diamonds, and who deposited an infectious giggle into a baby. This Man who created life in the Garden of Eden, declared His purpose for coming to live among us in this one simple phrase, *"I have come that you might have life ... and that you might have it more abundantly."*

If that was the promise of the Man who is Life himself, why are we not experiencing it? Why are most days boring and dull versions of an existence that was meant to be glorious and rare? Where is the abundance promised to us by the Giver of all good and perfect gifts?

Life in Spite of and Not Because of

There is an extraordinary historical account of a woman who was overweight her entire adult life and never married, although she longed for a home, a husband, and children of her own. She lived at home with her parents and older sister while working in the family business.

The one bright spot in an otherwise mundane week was teaching the special needs Sunday school class at church. Although this spinster never gave birth to children of her own, her delight was to teach these little ones who were never able to sit still and would never be accepted into a university. She taught these children with Down syndrome how to worship like David with their hands high in the air, dancing erratically around the cramped

Sunday school classroom, and singing off-key at the top of their small, but very loud, lungs.

This enthusiastic teacher taught the children how to be brave like Daniel and to look for angels rather than at lions.

Corrie, this Dutch heroine, taught these sweet little minds and hearts that God always takes care of His children and that, like Moses, when others are unkind to God's people, God will lead them into His promised land.

This courageous middle-aged woman of the 20th Century found delight in entertaining missionaries and other friends from church in her parents' simple home. They often enjoyed sharing a meal and then entering into a raucous evening of playing games followed by a reverent time of singing hymns and reading the Bible together.

Although never a mother, this woman had deep maternal longings and thus her favorite person in life was her nephew, Peter, named after the bold fisherman who loved Jesus without reserve.

Whenever she battled loneliness, she would offer to babysit one of the children in her Sunday school class so the tired parents could have a well-deserved night off.

This vibrant woman, in spite of her weight, her marital status, never traveling outside of her own village, and living with her elderly parents until in her mid-fifties, had discovered the secret of abundant life at its finest. She embraced the life she had been given and turned it into a valuable and breathtaking masterpiece of living.

Foundational Living

"The thief comes only to steal and kill and destroy; I came that they may have life, and have it abundantly" (John 10:10).

In this familiar and comforting verse, Jesus declares emphatically that the central purpose for His time on Earth can be summed up in one word: *Life!* Jesus came to deliver Heaven's idea of living to all of humanity for all generations to come. He did not guarantee perfect circumstances, but He promised more life than is necessary in the natural realm of understanding.

Obvious, also, in this verse is that there are two forces working against one another as you endeavor to live your life well. There is a thief whose chief desire is to steal your ability and your desire to tap into abundant life. His malicious intent is to kill your hope of an abundant life and then to destroy your abundant life at its very core. It is the only thing this archenemy of God knows how to do and it is the one pervasive thought on his ugly, deceitful brain. The goal of this insipid, ruinous wimp is to decimate the glory of your life with his attempt to have you settle for a life that is ordinary at best. This liar has no reason for existing other than to steal what God has planned for you this side of Heaven. The only tricks he has up his dirty, rotten sleeve are deception, lying, and falsehoods. Will you believe him or not? This skeletal shadow of a character endeavors to deceive you out of an abundant life. It is vital that you determine not to even listen to his senseless chatter, but to build a life firmly on the foundation of the truth found in the Word of God.

God has an abundant life for you that the death of Jesus Christ set into motion and ultimately guaranteed. This too-good-to-be-true life actually began the miraculous and eternal instant that you accepted Jesus into your heart as your Lord and Savior.

"Lord Jesus, I am a sinner and I need you. I believe you died on the Cross for my sins. Please forgive me for my sins. I thank you for the blood that you shed for me and I thank you for forgiving me of all of my sins. I thank you for rising from the dead so I could live forever with you. I ask you, Jesus, to come into my heart and live inside of me. I ask you, Jesus, to change me and my desires. I thank you, Jesus, for the gift of abundant life! Amen."

And with that resolute "Amen," the abundance of life begins!

The Artful Dodger

That simple and childlike prayer guarantees your access into all of Heaven's power and ushers in the possibility of experiencing peace in every storm that life may bring. You have been promised joy in the middle of deep and torturous sorrow and the ability to live in righteousness in spite of being placed into a world of moral compromise. Oh, there will still be too many days to count when life is hard ... outrageously hard ... but Christ has now delivered the intangible tools to you that will enable you to overcome the difficulties of life this side of Heaven.

And because you live in the war zone of mankind, the battle continues between the Giver of all Life and the father of all lies. However, what the deceiver has refused to face and has been in denial about since the Cross concerns this one major detail of eternal consequence—he has been soundly and eternally defeated! Christ, the Man of Life, is the ultimate Victor and His purposes are accomplished and now reign in eternity. Earth is the battlefield and Heaven is the victory lap. Earth is the place where confrontation reverberates and demons rattle their unbreakable chains. Heaven is where the roar of triumph echoes across the eons of unmeasured time!

Although defeated and rendered powerless, Satan continues to deceive, to fantasize, and to lie. He lies to you and about you; it is his only weapon of mock warfare. He tries to deceive you into believing that everyone else is living an abundant life but you. He lies and torments you with comparisons, futile competition, and half-truths birthed in fiction. The devil relentlessly endeavors to convince the sons and daughters of God that although Heaven is promised, life on Earth is sure to be bitter. He screams with hellish glee when he succeeds in convincing a believer that it is impossible to live an abundant life while sitting in the cesspool of circumstances.

The Greek word that describes the thief in John 10:10, is the word *klepto,* which was used to identify a bandit or pickpocket who was so skilled in his craft of stealing that his exploits of thievery were nearly undetectable. The type of thief Jesus was referring to in this portion of Scripture is the type who can slip his greedy little hand into the pockets of your life, take whatever his ugly little heart desires, and be long gone before you even realize what you are missing. Jesus used this particular word to describe the character and job description of the enemy so we would understand that the devil is incredibly cunning. The devil is dumb, but he is nobody's fool. He is not going to jump up and down and announce his presence in your life. Old klepto is not going to sit you down and warn you that he is about to invade your life and steal something rich and vibrant from you. He is a nocturnal creature who comes in when you least suspect it, silently and slyly steals from you what you value the most, and then slips away into the night of blackness and sin.

Perhaps you have been overwhelmingly busy lately and your life is ricocheting from one demand to another. Caring for aging parents, concern about one of your children, working full-time, and heavily involved in church activities fill every waking minute of your daily grind. Due to numerous activities and demands that relentlessly and loudly call your name, you have not read your Bible lately and might mistakenly think, "Well, God will understand that I am just too busy. I have read the Bible my entire life and in this season there is just not time. I am relying on the foundation I have built in the Word of God to get me through these busy, busy days." As you whip through this period of unremitting and sweaty busyness, your husband begins to get on your nerves and you begin to realize how uncaring and unhelpful he can be. With overwrought emotions out of control and no consistent daily spiritual strength to draw from, you begin to justify short, cold answers to his questions and then you strike back in undeserved anger and frustration. Strife has been birthed in your home because klepto has stolen your peace, your joy, and even your hope, and thus has clouded your dearly held and long-loved convictions about marriage. Klepto has an uncontrollable urge to get his hands into someone else's life so he can escape with that which does not and will not rightfully ever belong to him. Jesus has warned you that the devil is intent on stealing your life from you before you can even say, "Abundant!"

If you are beginning to realize you have not been living even half of an abundant life, guess who has been up to his criminal and rotten tricks at your expense? A career thief never dabbles in petty trinkets but has an eye for that which is of most value to the owner. A savvy pilferer does not bother to break into your house and then carry away what has only been purchased at the dollar store. He silently picks locks and proceeds to carry out heirlooms, jewels, cash, credit cards, and electronics. Your enemy, otherwise known as the bandit, tries to sneak into your life and steal what is the most valuable from your ability to live an abundant life. He greedily devours your peace about the future and then embezzles your hope for God's goodness in your life. He snitches the joy that enables you to walk through sorrows and trials and finally shoplifts your moral purity.

There is a strong and powerful way to place an impenetrable lock on your life so this dirty, rotten criminal is unable to trespass. The Word of God will secure your life and guarantee that klepto is no longer able to pick the lock of your heart. You need to so saturate yourself with the Word of God on a daily basis that it becomes a high power security system through which no one is able to invade.

Not only does klepto come in to steal your abundant life but he is also intent on convincing you to willingly sacrifice it into his greedy little hands. The word for *kill* in John 10:10 is actually a very specific Greek word that is best translated *sacrifice*. The devil does not have the power to kill you, so instead his wicked strategy consists of trying to get you to sacrifice your abundance to him. He is deceiving you by convincing you that your circumstances are the determinate as to whether it is possible for you to live a life of abundance or not. The devil despises the fact that you are the beneficiary of the blessings of God and if he is unable to swindle and run with your abundant life, he will endeavor to convince you to literally sacrifice it to him.

As a last ditch effort of twisted resolve, this toothless, empty shell of demonic vapor will finally try to destroy or ruin your abundant life. He blows in with hot air, empty breath, and circumstantial evidence in order to trash and devastate everything within your sight. At moments like this, you must always remember that the faithful of God never walk by sight but always by faith.

Your Lifeline

"I came that they may have life, and have it abundantly," were the stirring and purposeful words of Jesus spoken to His band of brothers at one of His most intense teaching sessions chronicled. When Jesus spoke to His twelve handpicked disciples in this moment in time, He was thinking about you. He was thinking about me.

Jesus zeroed in on the length of the promise in this verse as He declared that His disciples would not only be given abundant life, but they would continually possess it. There is no expiration date attached to His promise of abundant life and it comes with no circumstantial conditions. Whatever you are facing today, the promise of abundant life is focused on you. Whatever your circumstances consist of does not determine your ability to be the recipient of this substantial promise made by the One who is Truth and Life.

In good times and in hard times ... in storms and in sunshine ... whether you are married or single ... whether you have ten children or are barren ... whether you are an empty-nester or a young mom ... whether you are a widower or a groom ... whether you are on food stamps or have a million dollar bank account ... you are the recipient of all of the benefits of this promise of continual abundant life.

In the Greek, there are three types of life that are each identified by a completely different word.

Bios life is the duration of your life. It is the dash on your tombstone as determined by exactly how many days you breathed in the oxygen of planet Earth. One receives bios life from one's cell structure, DNA, and bodily systems. The word bios is not used in John 10:10.

Psyche life consists of your mind and your intellect. This type of life is the knowledge you accumulate while on your life's journey and is encompassed by the books you have read, the degrees you have earned, the television shows you have watched, or anything else that delivered information which is now stored on the hard drive of your brain. Psyche life also encompasses the life that is lived in your soul, which is the seat of your feelings, affections, desires, and personality. One receives psyche life from the knowledge of others and is developed by how much time is spent reading, learning, listening, and watching. The word psyche is not used in John 10:10.

The third type of life in the Greek is *zoe* life. Zoe refers to the intensity of life and is always associated with living heartily and with gusto. Zoe life is how well you live and is demonstrated through your vitality and animation in response to life. Zoe life is not inherited from a genetic pool and is not taught through the knowledge of others. Zoe life comes from one place and one place alone: zoe life is a gift from God! Zoe life is fertilized in the presence of God and by cultivating the intimacy that comes from a relationship with the Lord of all lords. Zoe life thrives when a believer spends time in the Word of God and in worship. Zoe life flourishes when a man or woman of God determines to have a vibrant and active prayer life.

Zoe life is the highest and noblest form of life and is comprised of all the highest and best which the saints possess in God.

Zoe is joy ... righteousness ... peace ... purity ... and hope. Zoe is faith ... revelation ... wisdom ... and strength. All of those attributes, and more, are yours simply because you belong to Jesus. Jesus never meant for His children to live a pious and boring existence, but He came to show us how to live, and then to give us the methodology and promise of Life with a capital L!

Zoe life has nothing to do with your personality; psyche life encompasses your personality. Zoe life is pure gift ... it is an indescribable, unable to be returned donation from Heaven's eternal excess aimed at you today.

When Jesus gives anything, He gives it lavishly and generously. Whatever Jesus is, He is filled with that characteristic infinitely and eternally. Jesus is the greatest and most extravagant source of Life that ever has been or that ever will be. There is no form of life, neither bios, nor psyche, nor zoe, that was not birthed in Him.

Jesus not only came to Earth so that you, the object and recipient of all He is and all He has desired, could receive eternal life ... but so you could live an abundant life ... a meaningful life ... a miraculous life ... a magnificent life birthed in the heart of God from the beginning of time and captured in your finite heartbeat.

The life that Jesus came to Earth to bring to all of mankind is unable to be measured in human calculations. This life is more than remarkable in every way and is more life than one person is able to live during their bios life. God has added super abundance to your meaningless, vagabond existence so that no longer are you shackled by the same issues and events which paralyze people who are only living a psyche and bios life. Zoe life is extravagantly more than mere psyche and bios but it is life with the sparkle of Heaven stirred in.

Your life was never meant to be ordinary nor was it meant to be mundane. Your life was always meant to be a miraculous demonstration of the power of God manifesting itself in mere mortals. This is *your* life! Jesus came to give you *zoe* life and because of Him and all that He has packed in you ... you are so much more than remarkable!

What a Difference!

When these two phrases in John 10:10 are juxtaposed, it is obvious that the devil wants you to be defeated ... but that's not going to happen. You have been empowered with zoe life to defeat the devil. The accuser of the brethren desires for you to struggle emotionally and spiritually your entire bios life ... but that's not going to happen. You have been identified by zoe life as an overcomer and as more than a conqueror. The dastardly deceiver "says" that you are sick, depressed, down in the dumps, glum, and miserable ... but that's a lie from the pit of hell itself! We are a people who are filled with the joy of His presence. The one who pretends he knows how to roar wants you to be intimidated out of walking in your destiny ... but that's not going to happen. We are a people who thrive knowing that *all things work together for good to those who love the Lord* ... the Giver of Life!

Life in Spite of, not Because of

The dear, special-needs children, whom Corrie loved ferociously, began to disappear out of her weekly Sunday school class. One by one they ceased to show up for their favorite hour of the week. They were being taken by the government from their parents and placed in state institutions. Corrie's heart was broken not only for herself, but also for the distraught and lonely parents.

Shortly after the children began to disappear from their homes, Corrie's father gathered the family around the table one night and informed them that the ten Boom family would be making some serious changes. They were going to build a hidden room upstairs in their home and would be having some visitors who would be living in this hiding place. The ten Boom family was a Christian family of conviction and honor and were joining the ranks of hundreds of others who were assisting the Jews. The Jews in Holland were being sent to concentrations camps under one of the most evil regimes of all time.

By the end of World War II, this one family, the family of Corrie ten Boom, had saved over eight hundred Jews, as well as hundreds of Dutch underground workers.

The ten Boom family was betrayed and on February 28, 1944, the Gestapo arrived and took six members of Corrie's family to prison. Although the violent Gestapo ransacked the entire home and systematically searched everywhere, they never found the secret room where six Jews remained in hiding. These Jews were rescued by the Dutch Resistance nearly forty-seven hours later.

Everyone in Corrie's family, except Corrie herself, died in the concentration camps. She was the sole ten Boom survivor of this horrific injustice and she came home alone to live again. Thus began Corrie's life-long ministry around the world. Corrie testified everywhere she traveled:

"There is no pit that God is not deeper still."

"God gives us the love to forgive our enemies."

"Jesus always wins the final victory!"

When I was on staff at Oral Roberts University in the late 1970s, Corrie came and spoke to over 3,000 students in chapel. At the close of the service, the chaplain of the university, Bob Stamps, told me to quickly go to his office and retrieve Corrie's coat for her. She was tired after speaking and they wanted to whisk her out the back door of Christ Chapel.

I ran down the empty corridor to Brother Bob's office, identified Corrie's coat, and gathered it up in my arms. It was a gray, dingy, wool coat with a matted fur collar. Her winter coat was so worn and out of date I wondered if Corrie had had this particular coat since before World War II. As I rushed through the halls to make my way to the back of the chapel, I heard the Holy Spirit tell me to stop.

In the empty hallway, while Corrie still prayed for the thousands of students, I wrapped myself in her outdated, worn mantle and was bold enough, as only the young are, to ask the Holy Spirit for a double anointing of what had been given to Corrie.

Corrie ten Boom tramped for the Lord for thirty-three years until she was eighty-eight years old. She only retired after a stroke that took her speech. Corrie could no longer speak in English or in Dutch, but could still pray out loud in her prayer language.

Corrie died on her ninety-first birthday on April 15, 1983. Although Corrie was not Jewish by birth, she protected and cared for the ancient people of God. The Jews have a long held belief that only truly blessed people die on the day of their birth.

Corrie knew how to embrace the life that Jesus promised in John 10:10. She could have been a depressed, lonely woman lacking any true purpose in life. But instead Corrie gave all she had to give, loved when others hated, and gave cup after cup of cold water in His name to the children under her charge and a war-torn world.

Live for Legacy

How will you be remembered? Will you be remembered as a person who continually complained about his or her lot in life? Will you be paralyzed by depression and bitterness because of circumstances you hate and would never have chosen?

Or, because of John 10:10, will you determine today to live the life of God's dreams for your life? Will you embrace opportunities to serve, to love, and to give? Will you discover, like Corrie, that circumstances are merely the springboard for a destiny filled with the abundance of the One who is Life himself?

Prayer for Life

"Dear Jesus, I love You so much. Thank You for being the Author and the Giver of all life. I pray today that You will give me the strength to tap into the abundant, overcoming life You promised in John 10:10. I refuse to listen to the enemy and I determine to no longer be trapped by my circumstances or failures. Thank You for abundant life! In Jesus' name I pray, Amen."

Declaration of Life

"I declare that I am the recipient of abundant life. Jesus came to Earth to give me more life than I can ever imagine or hope for. I will live in the abundance of His nature and His plans for my life today and every day."

Scripture for Life

"The thief comes only to steal and kill and destroy; I came that they may have life, and have it abundantly" (John 10:10).

Words of Life

"It's not my ability, but my response to God's ability that counts." — *Corrie ten Boom*

CHAPTER 2

A Bigger Shovel

AS a boy growing up in the latter part of the 19th Century, Bobbie was described as restless, inquisitive, energetic, stubborn, and fanatically determined to amount to absolutely nothing. His temperament strongly clashed with that of his unrelenting father's and it seemed that Bobbie's back got stiffer and stiffer as he entered his teenage years.

As the biggest hulk in the seventh grade class, Bobbie was also the dumbest. He came to hate school with a physical violence and wanted to break out the school windows and kick out the school walls.

Because Bobbie was never much interested in going to school, to the chagrin of his Christian parents, he left home at the age of fourteen and became an apprentice to an ironmonger. Bobbie studied mechanics from a correspondence course that had been given to him, although he never completed any assignments. Always ready to travel, Bobbie moved to California where he learned welding and became familiar with the application of electricity.

His temperament, however, continued to get him into trouble wherever he moved. After a foundry superintendent called Bobbie a "back-talk smart aleck," he became homeless on the streets of Portland, Oregon. At seventeen years old, this strong-willed man-child found himself big, dumb, broke, unemployed, and unemployable.

Money, IRA's, Fort Knox, and the Price of Gold

Paul wrote the Books of 1 and 2 Timothy to a young believer, Timothy, who is the first "second generation" believer referred to in the New Testament. Timothy was a young man who was highly influenced by his mother, Eunice, and his grandmother, Lois, both of whom were Jewish believers who discipled Timothy in the home. Timothy was one of the young men who would carry on Paul's work after Paul was executed. Let's eavesdrop on a written conversation Paul wrote to his spiritual son Timothy, and to the young church at Ephesus.

> *Instruct those who are rich in this present world not to be conceited or to fix their hope on the uncertainty of riches, but on God, who richly supplies us with all things to enjoy. Instruct them to do good, to be rich in good works, to be generous and ready to share, storing up for themselves the treasure of a good foundation for the future, so that they may take hold of that which is life indeed.* (1 Timothy 6:17-19)

These three verses, written from a general in the faith, erase the option of riches being a prerequisite to the possibility of living a life of abundance and meaning. This is a vital topic to address when attempting to define *abundant life* to an audience of chiefly Western believers. We unfortunately believe, as twenty-first century Christians, that we are entitled to having it all and mistakenly presume that it is impossible to live a full and meaningful life without the benefit of gargantuan portions of money. Money is definitely a benefit and most of us certainly wish we had more of the green stuff, but never base your potential for living an abundant life on something as transient as your checking account. Never use your monetary lack as an excuse for living an inferior life.

One issue Paul clearly addresses in these verses is that the rich are not automatically experts at that which constitutes a life of abundance. Some of the most fulfilled people alive today don't have a penny to their names and yet they live a life full of Heaven's extraordinary abundance.

Pedestals and Principles

Twice in this section of Scripture, Paul uses the word "instruct" in the imperative form. This word, instruct, in the Greek actually implies something much stronger and more definitive than a mere classroom learning session. Paul was commanding Timothy to inform the rich of this world that they are required not to think more highly of themselves than they ought to think. The Holy Spirit, through the pen and heart of Paul, is declaring Heaven's opinion to those who are rich in the things of the world: You are no better than anyone else, so take yourself off your own pedestal.

Paul reminds the young Timothy, and the rich under his charge, that all riches are uncertain. This is the only time in the New Testament that this word "uncertainty" is used and Paul uses it to make a viable and eternal point. Paul is reminding those of us who love the comfort that wealth brings with it, that riches are absolutely unstable and that money can disappear as quickly as it can appear. There is no guaranteed way to invest one's earthly goods and riches in a worldly system of finance. Many people, at every historical juncture, woke up with great wealth but went to bed as mere paupers.

Do not erroneously believe that riches are a consistent source of *that which is life indeed.* The only thing riches seem to guarantee is there will always be something to worry about. Paul is addressing, in these sincere and vital verses, how important it is to separate who you are from what you own. As believers, we do not fix our hope on the uncertainty of riches but on God, the Giver of all good gifts. Whether one is hugely rich or devastatingly poor, we are all to fix our hope on God who is the rich One and who gives richly, extravagantly, and abundantly to those who are His own.

Abundant life is conceived and birthed from an intimate relationship with the Father and not from the treasures of this temporary planet. Although we are not to fix our hope on riches, isn't it amazing to know that we serve a loving and generous God who richly supplies us with all things to enjoy? God gives to us, His dearly loved children, things for our enjoyment, but not for our definition. God lavishly blesses His children with extravagance even in this life. He desires that we enjoy what we have been given and to recognize it as coming from His loving hand. If you are blessed with material wealth, have money in the bank, and consider yourself financially comfortable, enjoy it! Feel no guilt or shame for what you have been given. However, don't become conceited, and always remember to share everything you have been given.

Teamwork with God

"Who at anytime serves as a soldier at his own expense? Who plants a vineyard and does not eat the fruit of it? Who tends a flock and does not use the milk of the flock? ... the plowman ought to plow in hope and the thresher to thresh in hope of sharing the crops"
(1 Corinthians 9:7; 10b).

Part of the teamwork that occurs as we receive the abundant life Jesus promised, is that we co-labor with God during our days on Earth. God wants His children to work hard and then expect to be blessed. God wants us to invest our lives with diligence and with excellence in order that provision and even abundance of finances will be the result. God wants us to believe we will have enough resources to take care of our families and then to share with others. If your heart's desire is to experience the *life indeed* that Paul presented to young Timothy, then you will not fix your hope on the riches, but on the Giver of the riches *who richly supplies us with all things to enjoy.* And, when you are blessed in a material manner, you will enjoy what He has given to you.

The people of God have been especially empowered to receive

blessings from above, to enjoy the blessings that have been given to them and then to share everything God has generously given. One of the outstanding tenets of living the life of God's dreams for you is that abundance is certainly not measured by wealth, but by generosity.

Paul instructs his apprentice in the things of the Kingdom of God that after a wealthy person has enjoyed what God has given to them, then they must *do good, to be rich in good works, to be generous and ready to share.*

Part of the equation of living a zoe life of abundance, is to obey the call of the gospel to actively work hard at doing good deeds. It is true that doing good deeds does not save your soul, but doing good deeds is your faith at work in the lives of others. One of the central ways we are able to enjoy what God has given to us is by being diligent to bless others. When a believer understands the unequaled joy and wealth of sharing and generously making others' lives easier, they have certainly discovered the secret of living life well.

If you are a wealthy believer, you are not losing anything at all when you give away what you have to others. In truth, giving to others generously is the greatest investment package known to mankind.

If you are not a wealthy believer and find yourself envying those who have attained wealth, your goal is to keep your eyes on Jesus and not on what you do not have. There is undiscovered value in continuing to work hard and in faithfully giving and tithing what you possess to the Kingdom of God. There is deep fulfillment and delightful satisfaction in discovering ways to give to the Body of Christ that are non-financial in essence. When your bank account is too low to give to the missionary, volunteer to teach Sunday school. If you don't have stocks to cash in to give to the church building program, work in the nursery or volunteer to paint walls at church. God loves a cheerful giver whether the giver is supplying finances, strong muscles, or just a kind word.

Life Indeed!

"...storing up for themselves the treasure of a good
foundation for the future, so that they may take hold
of that which is life indeed"
(1 Timothy 6:19, emphasis added).

There is a guaranteed way for every believer to amass a fortune because there is a secure place, designated by God, where all investments are safe and are unable to be stolen or even diminished by time. Paul tells the younger and less experienced Timothy that there is a way to experience *life indeed!*

The safest place for all of your resources, whether they are financial, creative, your education, your home, your children, or your marriage, is to invest them in the Kingdom of God by blessing and then caring for others. The greatest use of your time spent on Earth is to spend it for something that will outlast your bios life. The wisest and most generous use of your resources is to invest them in the unshakeable Kingdom of God.

If your desire is to increase the size of your riches, the answer is to invest with God. If you want to assure that you will never again need to worry about finances, your wealth, a retirement fund, an investment portfolio, real estate, or family heirlooms, you will learn the security of building a solid foundation of giving to the Kingdom of God and the generosity of giving to others in your life.

When you are generous and always ready to share what you have in order to meet someone else's genuine need, you are building a foundation for your life that will be solid and will stand the test of time. This is the wisdom and secret of *foundational living.* A foundation plays a very definite role in providing unshakable stability for a structure and it is no accident that Paul used the word "foundation" to describe the impact that choosing to be generous has on the structure of your life. A foundation keeps a structure solid, no matter what is going on in the atmosphere or in the geography where the structure is placed. If you long to build a life of significance and a life that is solidly identified by its power to stand the tests of life, you will latch onto these verses, obey their instructions, and reap their benefits.

When you choose to be generous, regardless of your finances, you have tapped into one of the greatest secrets of living *life indeed*. Hoarders, although wealthy by the world's standards, know nothing of what it takes to live an abundant life. Selfish men and women, although financially secure and smugly in charge, have no idea what true living is all about. It is not riches that guarantee abundance, but it is a lifestyle of generous giving and reaching out to others.

Have you discerned what is truly important in life yet? It is to place all of your hope on the God who blesses His children enormously. It is not your ability to acquire riches and accumulate possessions that is the guarantee of a wealthy lifestyle. The most important investment you will ever make in your ability to leave a legacy to those who come after you is to open your home, your heart, and your checkbook and to give to those in need. Life at its core is lived best by someone who generously and consistently gives of their gifts, their resources, and their time. Intentional givers know the joyful truth that we are not here to amass an earthly kingdom, but to build a heavenly fortune!

"The richest people in life don't have the best of everything, they just make the best of everything."
— *Unknown.*

God's Shovel

Bobbie turned his heart away from pride and self and turned his heart toward the God of his parents. When Bobbie humbled himself and finally asked God for help, he realized God had been on his side all along. It was at the crucial moment of turning his entire life over to the God of creation that Bobbie found that God's hand had given him special talents and abilities that could not be measured in a classroom, but in the creativity of foundries, factories, and patents.

Robert LeTourneau was the inventor of the electric wheel and at his death held the patent for nearly three hundred other inventions. During World War II, this genius, who grew up floundering for purpose and fulfillment, produced 70 percent of the world's earth moving machines and always spoke of God as his Chairman of the Board. Robert gave 90 percent of what he made to missions, Christian education, and the church, and lived only on 10 percent of what he made. The formerly homeless and hungry teenager, now a grown man and world-renowned in business, said the money came in faster than he was able to give it away. LeTourneau was convinced he would never be able to out-give God, although he spent the rest of his life trying to do just that.

"I shovel it out," he would say, "and God shovels it back, but God has a bigger shovel than I do!"

This boy who was raised in poverty and spent his teenage years roaming from job to job on the streets of the West Coast, as an adult millionaire and philanthropist, chose as his life verse, *"Seek ye first the Kingdom of God and His righteousness and all these things will be added unto you"* (Matthew 6:33).

Prayer for Life

"Dear Jesus, I love You so much and I long to have Your perspective on riches, wealth, and giving. I pray that as You bless me with finances and material goods I will have the strength and generosity to attempt to out-give You! Use me for Your Kingdom at this time in history. In Your powerful name I pray, Amen."

Declaration for Life

"I declare that I will be a giver and not a taker. I declare that I will try to out-give God every day of my life. I declare that I will seek first the Kingdom of God and that I will experience the joy of life indeed!"

Scripture for Life

"But seek first the Kingdom of God and His righteousness and all these things will be added to you" (Matthew 6:33).

Words of Life

"In prayer we are occupied with our needs, in thanksgiving we are occupied with our blessings, but in worship we are totally occupied with God himself." — *A.P. Gibbs*

CHAPTER 3

The Greatest Love Story Ever Told

WOULD you still be a Christian without the promise of Heaven? Would you still ask Jesus into your heart and passionately serve the Lord if life ended at your final breath? If there were no guarantee of eternity, would you still spend the next five ... or ten ... or thirty ... or seventy-five years loving the Lord? If your answer to this valid, yet simple, question is an emphatic, "Yes!" then you have begun to experience the joy of life in its fullest measure.

All of Our Tears in a Bottle

Joseph Aaron's name is written in no history book but the one in Heaven. No newspaper has printed his story of traumatic pain and raw tragedy. But our God ... the Maker of all that is good and righteous and holy ... the God Who promised to hold all of our tears in a bottle ... has wept over the life of a man by the name of Joseph Aaron.

Joseph Aaron was the youngest of eleven children born to a German Jewish rabbi who had been married three times. His first two wives had died and his third wife was Joseph's mother. Joseph was only four years old when his father moved to Holland, leaving his mother to care for Joseph and his ten siblings. At six years old, Joseph and his sister, Rachel, were taken from their mother and sent to live in a German children's home. The rest of his family was taken to Auschwitz where his mother and nine other siblings were immediately killed in the gas chambers.

On the day Joseph was separated from his sister, Rachel, Joseph remembers hearing the whistle of a train and its engine roaring past him. He remembers locking fingers with his sister until German soldiers forced them onto two different trains.

Joseph was taken to a concentration camp where he had to clean railway tracks in the hot sun from dawn until dark seven days a week. Joseph's seventh birthday came and went with no celebration and no acknowledgement.

One day Joseph eyed a small, rotten potato on the ground and quickly picked it up to take a bite. A Nazi soldier yanked Joseph up from the ground and screamed in his little boy face, "Do not steal from the German people! You are a thief and I could kill you immediately!" The solider took a hammer from his belt and smashed Joseph's two big toenails and then ripped off the rest of his toenails. Joseph vomited from the excruciating pain while the solider threw him back at the railway tracks to continue working in the heat of the day.

Joseph remained in this railway camp for over two years, and when he was nine, he was dragged out of bed one morning with one hundred other young boys. They were forced to stand in a straight line, completely erect lest they be shot dead on the spot. As the boys were being thrown into military vehicles, Joseph and nine other boys were forced into a separate line. A soldier spat in their faces as he said, "They are all going to Auschwitz; however it is not time for you to die."

Joseph and the nine others were taken to a secluded spot far away from civilization. These ten boys were raped every day and every night for over two years. Soldier after soldier after soldier violently abused these boys.

After two years of physical and sexual torture, the drunken soldiers took the bruised, bleeding, and weakened bodies of the ten boys into a field and threw them in a pile. Singing and shouting, the soldiers smashed their bottles into thousands of glassy pieces and jammed the shards of glass into the skin of the emaciated boys. The boys were left, unattended and bleeding to death, for nearly three days.

On the third day, the bleeding, nearly lifeless heap of boys was found by a group of British soldiers. Only three of the boys were still alive. The British soldiers sobbed as they picked up the surviving children, held them in their strong, safe arms, and cried over their short, yet horrific, lives.

The surviving three boys were flown to Switzerland for treatment and Joseph Aaron spent over a year in the hospital. After being released, Joseph was taken to a children's home in Holland where eventually he was told he was being taken to live with his sister, Rachel.

Because of the deep trauma and emotional pain that had been inflicted on Joseph, he no longer remembered he even had a sister. After living with her for nearly a year, memories of their childhood together finally began to flood his broken soul.

Rachel and Joseph were then shipped to Israel as refugees, were given ten pounds each, and were told to find a way to make a living. Joseph did not know how to read or write, and he and Rachel lived on a park bench for nearly a year, eating out of the trashcans, and bathing in nearby ponds. One day, an elderly gentleman invited them to his home, fed them, allowed them to shower in his immaculate and spacious bathroom, and then to sleep that night in his clean beds. The next day, this benevolent and kind human being, took Joseph to the restaurant of a friend in order to find a job.

When the restaurant owner met with Joseph, he took one look at him and said, "How can I give this boy a job? He can't communicate. He can't talk. He can't read or write. He does not even know the alphabet or numbers."

The kind gentleman, who had so mercifully taken Joseph and his sister in, continued to beg the restaurant owner for a job for Joseph. Joseph quietly slipped out into the busy street, got on his knees, and began to beg Yeshua to help him. A miracle happened in that moment as Yeshua appeared to Joseph in the street and told him to return inside to speak with the owner. When the owner and Joseph's protector looked toward Joseph as he entered the restaurant, their eyes widened in disbelief. The owner grinned and said, "Joseph! You look different! Go begin taking orders! You have a job!"

The miracle that happened to Joseph not only changed his countenance and gave him courage, but it was also a miracle of knowledge. Joseph could instantly understand, write, and read in German, Dutch, Hebrew, French, and English.

"Through all the years of my tortured life, I knew that Yeshua was with me. He took care of me and protected me. He delivered me from evil. I have believed in Yeshua since I was a child even though my family did not believe. I always felt His presence and heard whispers of His name in the concentration camps. He gave His life for me and now I live my life for Him." (Taken from the journal of Joseph Aaron.)

The Relentless Journey

From the Garden of Eden to the blessing of Abraham ... from the Promised Land to the worship of David ... from the love story found in the Song of Solomon ... to the prophets who foretold of a coming Messiah ... from the birth of Jesus ... to Calvary ... to Pentecost ... God has been wooing His children. He has been aggressively and relentlessly courting them and revealing His heart of unconditional love toward them. For thousands of years of recorded history, God has been on an eternal journey across the ages to win your heart. And that, my friend, is what makes your life so abundant: His passionate pursuit of all that you are!

There is an undeniable romance that was birthed in the Garden of Eden and continues to this day. The God of Creation ... the Christ of the Cross ... the Holy Spirit of Pentecost ... will stop at nothing to romance you into relationship with them. The love story that began in Paradise culminates when you say, "I do!"

: "I do love you, Jesus."

: "I will serve you, Jesus."

: "I am yours forever. I belong to you and to you alone."

Women understand the joy of romance and the thrill that only is felt with a "happily ever after" ending. Women long for the fulfillment that follows being captured by the man of her dreams. What men understand is the chase ... and what women long for is the embrace. You are the main character, the pursued, the object of eternal love and undying affection in the greatest love story ever told! It is a love story of epic proportions at which angels gasp, so great is their desire to experience the love of the Father for His children.

Whetting Your Appetite

"I will make an everlasting covenant with my people, I will not turn away from following them to do good to them and I will put a desire in their hearts to worship Me and they will never leave Me"
(Jeremiah 32:40).

The goodness of God is indeed chasing you down every single minute of your human life on planet Earth! This verse, spoken by the prophet Jeremiah, declares that God never stops doing good to His children. The goodness of God is both eternal and perpetual; it is also not based upon how you act, but upon who He is. He is good and He loves being who He is. We don't deserve His goodness and yet He is good still—perpetually and eternally. His goodness creates an appetite in us to know Him and to respond to Him. You will never desire more of Him, or even any of Him at all, until you believe with your whole heart that He is entirely good.

In order to understand the depth and wealth of meaning that accompanies the promise of much more life than we could ever imagine, we first must embrace a burning conviction that He truly is enthusiastically good. All the time good! When you begin to understand how completely and eternally good God is, it is in that moment your heart will desire to belong to Him completely ... forever and ever. Certainly there will be other events, people, and circumstances that will attempt to divert your attention from His ultimate and total goodness, but these distractions will leave you empty and unsatisfied. You will realize you have been duped to travel a road away from the One who longs for your heart. There will be other goals, projects, and dreams that demand your attention for moments in time, but ultimately you will understand that the only pursuit in life with any meaning at all is developing a friendship with God. The love and adoration that is cultivated at the center of who you are will add magnificent meaning to every other pursuit in life. When you say a final and resounding, "*Yes!*" to God at the altar of self and promotion, you will find there is nothing else in life that is actually worth living for.

When we attempt to circumvent this relationship with God and replace His presence with other kingdoms and ruling powers, the frustration is massive and the emptiness echoes across the caverns of our souls. This longing for His ultimate goodness grows in direct proportion to the time spent in His presence. As we rest in all He is and all He does, as we read His thrilling love letter written to our hearts, and as we sing and weep in the adoration of worship, the appetite for Him is stirred by the reality of His presence.

There is no other created being who is called into intimate friendship with the King of creation. Human beings were singularly given the rapturous opportunity to respond to His beckoning and to His call. The love story that began as "Once upon a time in the Garden of Eden ... " will never culminate until you say, "I do!"

As in any love story, there are appointments and memorable moments. There are photographs of events and diary entries. So it is with the love story between you and God ... there have been recorded moments where His pursuit of you has been on display for all of eternity to observe. Let's time-travel through history and linger at scenic places where God declared, "You are mine! All that I have and all that I am is yours!"

It All Began Here ...

"Then the Lord God formed man of dust from the ground, and breathed into his nostrils the breath of life; and man became a living being" (Genesis 2:7).

The joy of an abundant life is first experienced when you feel the breath of God on your life. You will be alive in ways you have never been alive before when you place yourself in close enough proximity to feel His breath upon you and upon all that you do! You will be the recipient of more than enough life for one piece of humanity when His breath rests upon the beat of your heart. Life will luxuriously ooze out of your pores and splash onto the world around you. Why? Because your life has been touched by the breath of God. Linger there.

God created man in His own image, in the image of God He created him; male and female He created them. God blessed them; and God said to them, "Be fruitful and multiply; and fill the earth, and subdue it; and rule over the fish of the sea and over the birds of the sky and over every living thing that moves on the earth." (Genesis 1:27-28)

The very first action God performed after He created you was He blessed you. It has always been in the heart of God that the object of His great affection and devotion would ultimately live a life of grand blessing. The romance that has eternally been in the heart of God toward His children was now evident in full force in the Garden of Eden: He had breathed life into their very beings and had pronounced Heaven's blessing upon them.

Abundant life is not a principle conceived in a great conversation Jesus had with His boys one day, but it has been God's gift to His children since the very beginning of all recorded time. The life of Jesus was to restore what had been lost by sin and shame. He never meant that it was possible to experience abundant life without breath-to-breath contact with Him.

It's Time for a Change

"Now the Lord said to Abram, 'Go forth from your country, and from your relatives and from your father's house, to the land which I will show you'"
(Genesis 12:1).

Our second stop on the journey of romance with the God of creation is at a moment in history when God was having a conversation with a human being who has been identified as *"a friend of God"* (see James 2:23). God told Abram it was time for a change and for Abram to take his eyes off all that was familiar and safe. God was leading Abram away from the familiar and into a land where Abram would be blessed beyond what he currently knew. God was about to teach Abram the importance of discerning blessing beyond circumstance.

Although God told Abram he was going to leave his country of origin, He did not tell Abram where He was leading him. Abram was being called to leave his former, comfortable environment in order to cultivate his friendship with God. The friendship Abram was able to cultivate with the Giver of all life would be the standard for those of us who long for a divine relationship. God was teaching His friend that change fertilizes dependence upon His own character. Although we serve and love a God who never changes, He is also a God who loves to instigate and encourage change in His friends.

Many of us find ourselves in this place of uncomfortable transition and change where Abram was that day. Like Abram, it is vital to realize that in order to go deeper into relationship with the Lover of your soul, you need a transfer of dependence and of affection. God loves you and will continue to pursue you even if you refuse to transfer your dependence in a deeper way to Him. God will continue to be good to you even if you refuse the change He offers because He can be no other way than good. However, just as change was for Abram's highest and best, so it is for yours. There is a part of life you will never experience if you tenaciously cling onto all that is familiar and comfortable. You will be living a life at its absolute finest when you are fully dependent upon Him ... the One who never changes!

As those who are responding to the love He offers, we must retrain ourselves to love the eternal and not the temporary. We must learn the joy of walking by faith and not by the familiar. We must follow Him onto roads and pathways unknown, knowing He is all we ever need.

> *"And I will make you a great nation, and I will bless*
> *you, and make your name great; and so you shall*
> *be a blessing"* (Genesis 12:2).

God is chasing you down in order to make you into something you could never possibly be on your own. God has blessed you and then He has named you "blessing"! You have been chosen to be a source of God to your world; you are a gift to history at this moment. Your life is a present, wrapped in God's love, delivered with God's blessing as a rare and valuable treasure that reveals His heart.

> *Now when Abram was ninety-nine years old,*
> *the Lord appeared to Abram and said to him,*
> *"I am God Almighty; walk before Me and be*

*blameless. I will establish My covenant between Me
and you, and I will multiply you exceedingly." Abram
fell on his face, and God talked with him, saying, "As
for Me, behold, My covenant is with you, and you
will be the father of a multitude of nations. No longer
shall your name be called Abram, but your name
shall be Abraham; for I will make you the father
of a multitude of nations. I will make you exceedingly
fruitful, and
I will make nations of you, and kings will come forth
from you." (Genesis 17:1-6)*

This is abundant life from Heaven's perspective! It is the promise of God's entry into and blessing upon all of our life's circumstances. This is the covenant relationship from the Lover to the Beloved, "I will remain in relationship with you and will multiply you exceedingly. All that I am and have is for your highest and best all the days of your life. Because of My love for you, you will become more than you could ever be on your own."

When Abram finally fell on his face before God and responded to the friendship with God who had been pursuing him, God changed Abram's name. God breathed into Abram's life the breath of Yahweh, which is the breath of God. The *ah* sound that is birthed from the identity of Yahweh has now settled into Abraham and has changed his identity forever. Because Yahweh blew His breath into Abram's life and because Abram responded by falling on his face in the presence of the Pursuer, Abraham will now be multiplied into eternal impact, significance, and fruitfulness.

The same thing will happen to you when you fall on your face in His presence and allow Him to breathe His breath into your life. God will breathe His very identity into you; your potential for greatness suddenly becomes the reality by which you live.

Face-to-face Friendship

"Moses went up to God, and the Lord called to
him from the mountain, saying, 'Thus you shall say
to the house of Jacob and tell the sons of Israel'"
(Exodus 19:3).

Moses went up to the high places of God to respond to His call and His offer of friendship and intimacy. Have you been to the high places of God in response to all that He is and all that He offers in relationship? It is in that high place of worship and submission that you, like Moses, will hear His voice. It is in that high place of adoration and surrender that you, like Adam, will feel His breath upon you. It is in that high place of praise and awe that, like Abraham, you will become more than you could ever be on your own.

'You yourselves have seen what I did to the Egyptians,
and how I bore you on eagles' wings, and brought
you to Myself. Now then, if you will indeed obey
My voice and keep My covenant, then you shall be
My own possession among all the peoples, for all the
earth is Mine; and you shall be to Me a kingdom of
priests and a holy nation.' "These are the words that
you shall speak to the sons of Israel." (Exodus 19:4-6)

These verses describe the heart of the Deliverer to His people and also detail the plans He has for them. He is a God of relationship and protection for those He loves; His kind intent is that His beloved would rule for Him among the people. The resulting factor of romance is abundance in His presence.

"Thus the Lord used to speak to Moses face to face,
just as a man speaks to his friend" (Exodus 33:11).

The Lord spoke to Moses simply because they were friends,

which resonates within all of us as abundant life at its finest. Having God consider you as His very own friend, as someone He loves, and as an intimate companion is truly the most magnificent aspect of life this side of Heaven. All other friendships pale in comparison, all other experiences fade on the horizon, and all other pursuits seem trivial in comparison. Never cheapen the value of abundant life and mistakenly place it in the same category as Disney and dollars and diamonds. You, as the object of His undying love, have been selected to cultivate a friendship with God.

But whenever Moses went in before the Lord to speak with Him, he would take off the veil until he came out; and whenever he came out and spoke to the sons of Israel what he had been commanded, the sons of Israel would see the face of Moses, that the skin of Moses' face shone. So Moses would replace the veil over his face until he went in to speak with Him.
(Exodus 34:34-35)

When Moses came out from meeting with the Lord, the skin of his face had a radiance about it that was visible to all with whom he came in contact. The people, also, who come in contact with you should see the remnant of the divine romance on your face. Your time in His presence should seep out of the earthly pores of your life and nearly be inexplicable to the world. When you slow down enough to be an intimate friend of God and choose to go to the high places of His presence, it will change your countenance, your influence, and how the companions of this world perceive you. Abundant life was never meant only for you, but it was meant to impact those who gather around your life. Face-to-face contact with God is the greatest difference-maker you will ever experience. It trumps counseling sessions, prestigious education environments, rubbing shoulders with the rich and famous, and well-worn passports. To behold God and to remain unchanged is humanly impossible!

Here Comes the Bride!

" ... as a bridegroom rejoices over his bride ...
so shall the Lord rejoice over you" (Isaiah 62:5).

When you love someone, really love someone, the priority instantly becomes spending time together in order to get to know the person better. The desire of your heart is to know this person from the inside out. A surface relationship holds no interest when you are deeply in love with someone and you long for more ... more ... more. This deep intimacy and knowledge of the object of your love is cultivated simply by spending time together. Communicating with your love, listening to your love, spending time with your love becomes the only thing that really matters in life.

May I simply remind you God has that wedding-day glow when He looks at you? You are the object of His eternal affection and when He sees you coming toward Him ... His heavenly heart just might skip a beat!

Unfortunately, many of us are way too busy to cultivate this relationship that is at the core of life itself. We mistakenly believe everything else is of much more importance than simply time spent in His dear presence. As you are on this extraordinary journey of learning how to love God while your feet are planted on terra firma, bask in the delight of simply enjoying His presence. Get to know Him and listen for His voice. Anticipate your moments together with heart-stopping expectancy.

Getting to Know You

"Let him who boasts boast of this, that he
understands and knows Me ..." (Jeremiah 9:24).

I have been married for nearly four decades and in that time, although I think I know Craig better than any other human being on planet Earth, there are still moments when I exclaim, "Why, I didn't know that about you!"

We are humans and finite beings and yet a lifetime is still not enough to truly know all of the facets of the love of your life.

When it comes to getting to know God, if you live to be 109 years old and spend your entire life on this incredible quest to know Him, you will only be acquainted with a minute piece of God's infinite and amazing character. If the goal of your life's journey is to know God, you must spend time reading His love letter that was written to you for just that very purpose.

When you determine to read your Bible regardless of your circumstances, you will be the recipient of a peace in your soul that is unable to be denied. When you daily spend time in the Word of God, a purpose will flood your being and you will be convinced of His great goodness toward you. Those who choose not to be in the Word of God on a consistent basis, although they are Christians and are headed for Heaven, are tormented by the issues of their lives. If you refuse to immerse yourself in the extraordinary missive of eternal perspective and wisdom, you will not have the power to fight depression nor the wisdom to make a righteous decision.

So many Christians use the excuse, "I don't understand the Bible. That's why I don't read it."

To that weak excuse of justification, I often reply, "Christians don't primarily read the Bible for information but for transformation."

When you read the Bible, a miracle happens in the deepest part of you; the powerful strengthening that occurs is that miracle.

The Bridegroom is so in love with you that He has written an eternal love letter from His heart to yours ... will you read it? Or will it grow dusty on some shelf cluttered with magazines and New York Times bestsellers? If you say that you are His friend, you will spend time getting to know Him. If you respond to His call of love, you will understand the value of who He is and what He has said.

The Power of Love

"Now as they observed the confidence of Peter and John and understood that they were uneducated and untrained men, they were amazed and began to recognize them as having been with Jesus" (Acts 4:13).

God's love for you, and His goodness toward you, is not earned based on the fact that you are an amazing person filled with gifts, talents, and abilities. God's absolute delight over your life is not because you ran a marathon, lost forty-seven pounds, or because you have been married for nearly thirty years. God's pursuit of you is not because all of your children are serving Christ or that you have earned three graduate degrees. It doesn't matter how much you weigh, what you know, or where you have been. He simply wants you ... He aches for your attention and for your heart so the world will recognize you as having been with Jesus.

I can never be content to live a mediocre existence having a substandard knowledge of the Man who has captured my heart. My heart races knowing there is more of God to explore than I have ever imagined, and my life will only be as abundant as the amount of time I spend with Him.

It has always been astounding to me that Jesus did not set limits on how much we could have of Him or know about Him in this lifetime. There is no end to the favor He has for your life and He does not have to give rain checks when it comes to His blessings because He never runs out!

It is a twisted spiritual mentality to believe that God has these sorts of opinions and expressions:

"OK ... I have blessed you enough ... I need to go on to the next one."

"OK ... You have read your Bible through seven times in the past four years. You never need to open it again."

"OK ... You have been to eleven conferences, fourteen prayer retreats, four marriage conferences, and thirty-two revivals. It's somebody else's turn. You have done enough"

"OK ... I have already healed you twice. Are you trying to be selfish or something?"

God's favor, first and foremost, is about giving us the grand privilege of knowing Him ... simply for the purpose of knowing Him!

Beautiful Things

A college missions team was invited to visit Joseph Aaron, the man who had endured atrocities in concentration camps during World War II. This man lived a quiet existence far from the glare of human interest, but was happy to share an afternoon with a group of young people who loved to worship Yeshua. Here is the end of Joseph Aaron's story in the words of my daughter, Joy, who was on the missions team invited to his humble yet lovely home:

"Our rickety van drove up a winding road to a remote building, far from civilization. Shingles were falling off the face of the building and explicit graffiti was strewn on every visible wall. We tripped over garbage cluttering the parking lot and stray cats as we approached the building.

Our contact led the way to Joseph's apartment and knocked on his door while we waited around the corner. After she sweetly and quietly greeted him, we were allowed to enter his worn, three-room apartment. He welcomed our team of eight Americans with literally open arms. As each one of us passed through the door, Joseph Aaron greeted us with kisses on our cheeks. Waiting for us in his tidy living room was a feast fit for a king or two! Homemade breads, cakes, fruit, coffee, and tea were set out for our pleasure. Besides my own home, I had never felt so welcome anywhere.

Joseph told us his life story and then recounted how after he was hired by the restaurant owner, he was able to earn a living for himself and Rachel. He lives only fifteen minutes away from his beloved sister, who is also still alive. Rachel is now a widow with three daughters who live around the world.

It brought humility to my heart when I realized that even though Joseph had been brutally tortured, his countenance is one of peace and forgiveness. He told us that he remembers the moment when Yeshua asked him to forgive the German people and that he holds no bitterness in his heart.

At the end of his testimony, Joseph asked us to sing over him. As we sang, I could almost hear the voice of God singing with us over Joseph Aaron.

These were the words of the song that we attempted to sing over him in spite of our sobs,

'All this pain ... I wonder if I'll even find my way.

I wonder if my life could really change at all?

All this earth, could all that is lost be ever found?

Could a garden come up from this ground at all?

All around hope is springing from this old ground;

Out of chaos life is being found in you!

You make beautiful things, you make beautiful things out of the dust!

You make beautiful things, you make beautiful things out of us.'

– Michael Gungor

I wept as I watched Joseph Aaron close his tear-filled eyes and listen to our song. Joseph truly knows how Yeshua makes beautiful things. He feels the breath of God upon his scarred face and soul."

The Value of Romance

The cry of my heart is that you will wonder no longer ... that you will never again question where abundant life begins. Life begins with expressed love and so abundant life actually began with the divine romance in the Garden of Eden. Any abundance you will ever experience will be given when you allow Him to breathe on you. The breath of Creation, the protection of the rainbow, the betrothal of the promise of the prophets, the miracle of the manger, the romance of Calvary, and the vow of Pentecost surround your life with a love so rich and strong that you are able to live a life at its finest and at its fullest. Love changes everything about your life today. Dance in His perfect love for you ... rest in His arms of joy and hope ... be dazzled with His gaze into your eyes ... and look forward to a future with the God who became Man to pursue you with His eternal love.

Prayer for Life

"Dear Jesus, I love You so much and today I respond to the call of Your love toward me. I will spend the rest of my life on Earth loving You, knowing You, and responding to Your goodness toward me. You are the delight of my soul and the object of my love. In Your beautiful Name I pray, Amen."

Declaration for Life

"I declare that I am the beloved in the greatest love story ever told. I declare that God's goodness is chasing me down every day of my life. I declare that friendship with God is the greatest treasure of my life."

Scripture for Life

"I will make an everlasting covenant with my people, I will not turn away from following them to do good to them and I will put a desire in their hearts to worship Me and they will never leave Me" (Jeremiah 32:40).

Words of Life

"God has, as it were, placed himself on display in the art gallery of the universe. He beckons His people, you and me, to stand in awe as we behold the symmetry of His attributes, the harmony of His deeds, the glory of His goodness, the overwhelming and unfathomable grandeur of His greatness; in a word, His beauty. God is infinitely splendid and invites us to come and bask in His beauty that we might enjoy Him to the fullest." — *Sam Storms*

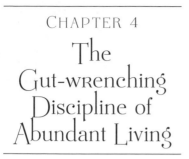

CHAPTER 4

The
Gut-wrenching
Discipline of
Abundant Living

BARBARA JOHNSON had an extraordinary life filled with the stuff of which most women only dream. Born in 1927, Barbara, as a young woman, married the man of her dreams, had four lively sons in succession, and by the early 1950s was living, literally, the great American dream. The Johnsons were active in their community and especially in their church as youth leaders.

The entire Johnson family was preparing to go with their church on the annual youth retreat in 1966 in the mountains of California. Barbara's husband, Bill, was driving alone while Barbara had the two youngest sons in the car with her. Their two teen-age boys were understandably riding with the youth group in the church van. About ten miles from the resort site, Barbara's headlights beamed on the figure of a large man lying in the middle of the mountain road covered in his own blood. Although he was unidentifiable due to his horrific head injuries, Barbara knew who he was because she had ironed the shirt he was wearing only hours ago. It was her beloved husband and best friend, Bill.

The prognosis was not good, but Bill lived through the unending night. The doctors gently told Barbara there was extensive brain damage and although he might live, the old Bill would be gone. After a week of vigilant prayers, the doctors informed Barbara that Bill was permanently and completely disabled. There was a possibility that he would be a blind vegetable for the rest of his life, never to leave the hospital. Barbara knew she served a God who delights in touching broken people and making them whole again, and so began Barbara's journey into deepening her faith.

Barbara and her family adopted Mark 10:27 as their life verse:

49

*"With men it is impossible, but not with God; for
with God all things are possible."*

One year later, after days of faith and failure, tears and
laughter, therapy both mental and physical, and a relentless belief
in a healing God, Bill returned to work as a full-time mechanical
engineer. He had been healed in spirit and in body!

For one short year, the Johnson family settled back
into a normal, but much more thankful routine. Then in 1968,
Barbara and Bill's oldest son, Steve, joined the U.S. Marines and
was sent to Vietnam. Steve loved the Lord with his whole heart
and although the parting was painful, it was also peaceful. On July
28, 1968, the Johnson family learned that their eldest son was safe
in the arms of Jesus.

In the summer of 1973, Tim, their second son, took off
in a Volkswagen with two friends to "find himself." They spent
the summer wandering through Alaska and not only did Tim find
himself, he also found Jesus Christ. Tim joined a church fellowship
in Alaska, was baptized there, and gave his testimony one night
in church. Tim was a changed young man who was now filled
with the Holy Spirit, and with purpose and direction. The desire
of Tim's heart was to come home at the end of the summer and
to rebuild some bridges he had unfortunately burned. The new
Tim wanted to spend time with his parents and with his two
younger brothers.

On the night of August 1, 1973, Tim's blue VW was in a head-
on collision with a drunk driver who was on the wrong side of
the road. Tim was instantly ushered into the arms of his Savior.

In June of 1975, Barbara and Bill discovered that David, their
third son, had embraced a gay lifestyle and he then disappeared
into the gay community for eleven years with no contact at all
with his family.

How does a woman, a mother, go through such horrendous
circumstances and not lose her mind? If your name is Barbara

Johnson, you start a joy box. Barbara's joy box was just a little shoebox that she began to fill with things that brought her joy. When a note from a friend arrived in the mail, she would put it in her joy box. When she found a Scripture verse that was particularly comforting, she would write it on a card and put it in her joy box. She found a book of jokes from when the boys were little and stuffed that in her, by now, overflowing box. The spring flowers from the yard went in along with a favorite recipe or two.

When her pieces of joy outgrew the shoebox, Barbara bought a plastic tub and began filling the tub with little pieces of life that stirred up joy. When her joy memorabilia no longer fit in her dozens of bins, she emptied their guest bedroom and it became her joy room. When the guest bedroom could no longer hold it all, Bill built an addition onto their California ranch home to fit all of the notes, the poems, the music, the pictures, the Scriptures, and the mementos that reminded Barbara and Bill that they served a God of joy.

The Multiplication Factor

*"Grace and peace be multiplied to you in the
knowledge of God and of Jesus our Lord"*
(2 Peter 1:2).

As you get to know God and His Son, Jesus, in greater ways, grace and peace will actually reproduce themselves in your life. Grace and peace will multiply their presence in your life just by spending time with God and Jesus. If you want more peace, what you really need is more of Jesus. Peace is not the changing of your circumstances, but it is the changing of your mind and heart simply because you are intent on knowing every aspect of the character of Jesus.

Don't make this more difficult than it actually is ... getting to know Jesus in the deepest part of you is not extremely difficult, but neither is it especially simple. You must resolutely choose to know Him with every fiber of your being. He is longing for time with you and patiently waiting for your attention and for your interest. Every day, spend time with Him in the Word of God. There will come a moment in your daily walk with the Lord when reading the Bible will change from drudgery to accepted discipline. There will also come a moment in your pursuit of Him that reading the Bible as a daily habit changes from discipline to anticipated delight.

The most productive and fulfilling moments of your life will occur at the time when you choose to lift your hands and your heart in worship in His beautiful presence. At these moments, sing out loud and then say sweet and endearing words to Jesus just like you would to a friend or a family member. You shouldn't have to pretend He is with you ... because He really is with you in that moment! So pay attention to Him. Ignoring Jesus while professing to love Him is a serious violation of relationship.

One of the most practical habits and joyful choices you can make on this journey of knowing Jesus is to discover the delight of a prayer journal. This journal will welcome your daily prayer requests and celebrated answers; you can write down what God is teaching you and what you hear Him say to your heart. As the years fly by, and they will, you will have a living record of the fingerprint of God upon your life.

You can be as close to God as you desire to be; there is no limit as to how well or how deeply you can know Him. He never holds himself back from a disciple who genuinely pursues Him with heartfelt and reckless abandon. There is no gate around His presence that locks you out nor is there a fence around His power that boasts of a "Do Not Disturb!" sign. God does not dole himself out in daily increments and then coolly proclaim, "That is enough for today. You have had enough of me for today." There is no end to the intimacy you can experience with Christ so pursue Him passionately!

It is not *what* you know about God that ushers you into the possibility of abundant life, but it is simply to know Him. It is knowing the *Who* of God that gives your life the scintillating possibility of living abundantly and the exciting resolve to live way beyond the mundane. Spending a lifetime truly getting to know Jesus is the best invitation you have ever received. You have been given a ticket that ushers you into a front row seat of experiencing His live presence and His daily power. There is nothing mundane or boring about that!

It is interesting to note in the letter Paul wrote to Timothy, he said, *"I know whom I have believed ..."* rather than "I know *what* I have believed." (See 2 Timothy 1:12.) The *Who* of His presence is more important than the *what* of only a knowledge-based religion. Often when we pray for peace, beg for peace and then tell God everything He can do to deliver peace into our lives we have forgotten that the Bible has given to believers in every generation the instruction on how to arrive at a solid place of peace: know Him and trust Him. Peace is a by-product of trusting His character.

"The steadfast of mind You will keep in perfect peace, because he trusts in You" (Isaiah 26:3).

Everything!

"Seeing that His divine power has granted to us everything pertaining to life and godliness, through the true knowledge of Him who called us by His own glory and excellence" (2 Peter 1:3).

Peter and the Holy Spirit are reminding all of us who love Jesus that when we truly know Him in His fullness and power the blessings are nothing short of enormous! This phrase, *"His divine power has granted to us everything pertaining to life and godliness ..."* certainly must be one of the most compelling and potent phrases in the entire New Testament. God's power ... the power that Heaven experiences ... the same power that raised Jesus Christ from the dead ... is at your human disposal. He gives His power, which cannot be defeated or frustrated, to you who live today to serve Him in the twenty-first century. *How magnificent is that?*

The word for *power* that is used in 2 Peter 1:3 is the Greek word *dunamis* which is the exact same power Heaven sent to raise Jesus from the dead. You have dunamis power inside of you because He is in you. You are the storage unit for Heaven's dunamis power and as such there should be no excuses as to why you are unable to live an abundant and joy-filled life. You have no excuses for living a life under the weight of your circumstances. You have no excuses why you deserve to whine and complain. You have no excuses for sin because you are one dynamite person! There is no grave that can hold you ... there is no circumstance that can cripple you ... there is no person who can paralyze you ... and there is no situation that can force you to sin because you are *dynamite*.

You should be going through life blowing things up! Because you have been given dunamis power, you should blow up circumstances that used to depress you. You should blow up sickness with faith. You should blow up worry with worship.

It is one thing to be powerful, but it is another thing altogether to be generous with that power. Jesus tells us what life is all about at its core and then enables us to live life the way it ought to be lived by giving us His very own power. He offers relationship birthed out of love and then prods us not to withdraw from the life He has given to us, but to triumphantly participate in this life with Him and with His power. I am in ... all the way! How about *you?*

"I can do all things through Christ who strengthens me"
(Philippians 4:13).

When you know Jesus and are the beneficiary of the power of His Holy Spirit, you have everything you could ever possibly require to live an overcoming life of peace and joy.

"His divine power has granted to us everything pertaining to life and godliness ..."

Anything and everything you could ever need to live life this side of Heaven has already been given to you because His power has been given to you. You've got it. You've already got it!

> If you need the power to love a difficult spouse ... you've got it.
>
> If you need the power to pray for a child to come home ... you've got it.
>
> If you need the power to believe for a financial breakthrough ... you've got it.
>
> If you need the power to trust for a physical healing ... you've got it.

The word for "life" that is used in this verse in 2 Peter, is the Greek word *zoe* which is the kind of life Jesus promised to all of His disciples in John 10:10. The dunamis power that has already been deposited inside of you gives you the ability to live abundantly and to live just like Christ dreamed you would live. This type of life honors Christ wholeheartedly. Zoe life is a not a life that is driven by self or by profane desire, but it is a life that reflects who He is and what His desires are.

There will be days when you might feel you have come up short of His plans for your life and this inadequacy might be reflected in saying the wrong thing, thinking the wrong thing, or giving into a fleshly desire. There may be moments in life when you refuse to give someone the benefit of the doubt or respond out of lack rather than out of blessing. In those moments, when your life falls short of zoe, you must back up two steps and, first of all, remind yourself that you know God. Secondly, remind yourself that you have the dunamis power of Jesus Christ inside of you. In that instant, run back to your source of peace and grace and throw yourself into His open and loving arms. Focus on Him again and listen for His voice. Ask for His power to manifest itself in your mortal body and your life will strategically change. He has given you everything you need to verify you will never fall short again.

Peter's Favorite Word

I have always admitted to being a "word-aholic." I love words ... new words ... archaic words ... trending words ... beguiling words ... descriptive words ... and even made-up words. I polled a group of my dynamite friends and simply asked, "What is your favorite word?" These were some of their responses:

Believe

Delicious

Stunning

Give and Forgive

Mom

Victory

Chocolate

Family

Christmas

Beach

One of my favorite words has always been "resilient." It's a word that sounds exactly like what it describes: springing back, rebounding; recovering readily from illness, depression, adversity, or the like; buoyant.

"For by these He has granted to us His precious
and magnificent promises, so that by them you may
become partakers of the divine nature, having escaped

the corruption that is in the world by lust"
(2 Peter 1:4).

Peter was the rugged fisherman who spoke before he thought, acted before he asked, and was bold enough to try to correct Jesus a time or two. Really, Peter? Correcting Jesus? Peter, like me, had a favorite word that he used often and emphatically. This impetuous, outspoken, opinionated disciple used one particular word no less than seven times in two very short books in the Bible. Would you like to know the word that rolled off Peter's tongue and pen often and with meaning? The word is "precious."

Precious is a word that mothers generously splatter when describing babies and bouquets and greeting cards. But a stubborn fisherman? A man that smelled like fish guts half his life and went about cutting off people's ears? *Precious?* Peter? What are you talking about?

Peter was a man who knew the value of the promises of God and he knew of no other way to describe them but by calling them what they were: precious. Peter was attempting, with the help of the Holy Spirit, to communicate the intrinsic value and long-lasting impact of that which is found in the Word of God. Peter, the man on a mission, shouts through the ages, "Don't take the promises of God for granted! Realize the purpose of His promises and hold them dear and close to your life."

When Christ came, the age of the Law was completed for all of eternity. The Messianic Age had dawned for all who dared to believe in His fulfillment of prophecy. The birth, life, death, and Resurrection of the Messiah changed everything for all people at every moment in history. His life promised eternal life, healing, forgiveness of sins, and the power to overcome. His death sealed the promises and His Resurrection trumpeted the promises! The promises of God are ours in the affirmative through His Son Jesus Christ. The Word of God promises and Jesus, the Son, delivers.

What are some of God's promises toward us who believe?

Our households would be saved.

God hears and answers our prayers.

Jesus sits at the right hand of the Father interceding for us.

Greater is He who is in me than He who is in the world.

I am a new creation in Christ. Old things have passed away.

I am no longer a slave to sin.

Death holds no power over me.

God is working all things together for my good.

His Word will brighten our steps and light our path.

Not only are these promises precious, but the Bible, which is the source of all truth, also describes them as magnificent. The promises of God are the greatest truths of all time and there is absolutely no accurate way to measure their impact on your life in the twenty-first century.

"... so that by them you may become partakers of the divine nature ..." The Bible promises that God's promises promise that you can share in God's very own nature. You can savor all He is and then marinate in it to the extent that you become it! You have the potential of ingesting His very personality and exhibiting His exact character. Your life becomes a place of demonstration of His fruit and His power. You are no longer like you ... because of the promises ... you are now like Him. He became what we are to make us what He is.

"... having escaped the corruption that is in the world by lust." Not only can we have the glorious opportunity to participate in all that He is, but He has also given us an escape clause. We are called to walk in the opposite direction most of humanity chooses to walk. His promises, which make us like Him, usher us away

from the compromise and corruption of the world. No wonder the world doesn't understand us ... they are going "that-a-way" while we are going "His-a-way!"

What we have just studied is merely the warm-up to the painful discipline of living a power-packed life in Christ. We have been doing the stretches in order to complete the marathon of living the life of His dreams for you. Now it is time to discover the joy of discipline and of obedience that Christ meant for you to participate in. Only you can determine whether or not you will endure the challenge in order to discover the abundance that was promised.

Back to Barbara

When a car accident nearly took Barbara Johnson's husband's life, she filled his hospital room with Scriptures, quoted the Word of God over him, and had her sons memorize Scriptures to pray over their beloved dad.

When her first son was killed in Vietnam, she reached out to other mothers who had lost sons and had a cassette tape made with Steve's life story on it. She sent this recording to other grieving mothers and ended Steve's story with the comfort of the hymn, "Safe In the Arms of Jesus."

When her second son, Tim, was killed, she spoke in church that very Sunday morning and the altar was filled with Tim's friends who gave their lives to Jesus.

When her son, David, disappeared for eleven years into the gay community, Barbara began Spatula Ministries to peel parents off the ceiling when their children break their hearts.

Barbara's books have sold millions of copies and she changed hundreds of thousands of people's lives because of her testimony and her refusal to give into depression and hopelessness. Her commitment to embrace joy at the very worst moments of her life took supreme diligence. But Barbara did it because of God's power that was given to her and because she knew Him intimately.

We all choose how to walk out our faith. My prayer is that you will choose the diligence that will enable you to press ahead in the face of insurmountable and seemingly impossible odds. My prayer is that you will step over hell with your face set like flint toward the Kingdom of joy and peace.

Prayer for Life

"Dear Jesus, I love You so much. I pray for Your dunamis power to infiltrate the broken and weak places in my life. I pray that the precious promises found in the Bible will change me from a sinful, weak person into a glorious demonstration of the character and strength of God. In Your powerful name I pray, Amen."

Declaration for Life

"I declare that I am one dynamite person. I declare that the precious and magnificent promises of God have changed me into a living and breathing demonstration of the character of God!"

Scripture for Life

Grace and peace be multiplied to you in the knowledge of God and of Jesus our Lord; seeing that His divine power has granted to us everything pertaining to life and godliness, through the true knowledge of Him who called us by His own glory and excellence.

For by these He has granted to us His precious and magnificent promises, so that by them you may become partakers of the divine nature, having escaped the corruption that is in the world by lust. (2 Peter 1:2-4)

Words of Life

"Faith is seeing light with your heart when all your eyes see is darkness." — *Barbara Johnson*

CHAPTER 5

Reality Bible

WELCOME to Reality Bible at its finest! We live in an age that yearns for something real and genuine ... something without pretense or politicking. Reality Bible is the definitive belief that the Bible is a book of great substance and presents an all-consuming yet fulfilling challenge at every moment in history.

Reality television has introduced America to an entirely new brand of entertainment without million dollar budgets, extensive sets, and high profile industry stars. What reality television does, with its tongue in its very successful cheek, is to invite the viewing public into the private lives of ordinary people with a bit of shock thrown in for good measure.

Reality television has introduced the salivating viewing audience to the dysfunction of functional families simply selecting their daughter's wedding dress, the hilarity and delight that accompanies massive families who could field their own football teams with plenty left over to sit on the bench, and the regime of swamp families who chew tobacco, play with 'gators, and desperately need a course in English grammar. This particular brand of television has also instructed the public how to remodel a home, plant a garden, what not to wear, and decorate unbelievable cupcakes all in thirty minutes or less.

The motivating purpose of reality television is that people really do want to know how to do life ... and how to do it well. People are curious to discover how others live and then to learn from their real-life successes and failures.

Reality Bible is based on much of the same premise. Christians want to learn how to do life well and they deeply desire to know what to do according to the principles found in the Word of God—and more importantly, what not to do. The glaring difference between reality television and reality Bible is that reality Bible calls all believers to get off the couch. Reality Bible is birthed in the truth that couch potato Christians will never make a lasting difference nor will they have the tools to live life exceptionally well.

Only the Diligent Need Apply

Ruth Bell was born on June 10, 1920, the daughter of medical missionaries in China. Ruth and her siblings were raised in the midst of the disease, agony, and disorder that a Civil War brings to a country. This young woman saw Christians murdered for the cause of Christ and some of her dearest missionary friends killed by brutal savages in China.

Her parents, in spite of the fear and instability of war, exercised a profound effect upon the development of Ruth's character and laid the foundation for the woman she would become. What this extraordinary girl witnessed in her family home, she willingly and diligently practiced for herself: dependence upon God in every circumstance, a delightful love for His Word, a deep concern for others above self, and an indomitable spirit always displayed with a smile.

When Ruth was thirteen years old, her parents believed it best to send her to a Christian boarding school in Korea. She was ferociously homesick and often days went by when Ruth was unable to either eat or drink, so great was her emotional despair. It was during these dark, solitary days she learned to overcome her loneliness and to take care of the needs of others.

When Ruth turned seventeen, her parents sent her to the States in order to attend Wheaton College during the years preceding and during World War II. It was there Ruth met her future husband and gave up her long-held dream of becoming a missionary because that was not his dream or call. She raised her five children, most days alone, on a mountaintop in North Carolina while her husband traveled the world for Christ.

Ruth's happiness and fulfillment did not depend upon her circumstances. She was a lovely, beautiful, and wise woman simply because early in life she had determined to make Christ her home, her purpose, her center, her confidante, and her vision. Ruth gave up her childhood dreams in order to serve her husband, her children, and her aging parents.

And Let the Pain Begin!

Now for this very reason, also, applying all diligence,
in your faith supply moral excellence, and in your
moral excellence, knowledge, and in your knowledge,
self-control, and in your self-control, perseverance, and
in your perseverance, godliness, and in your godliness,
brotherly kindness, and in your brotherly kindness,
love. For if these qualities are yours and are increasing,
they render you neither useless nor unfruitful in the
true knowledge of our Lord Jesus Christ.
(2 Peter 1:5-8).

You must determine to be a diligent person in order to enjoy the extreme benefit of living an abundant life that is not of your own making or choosing. Those who decide to jump into diligent living quickly discover this lifestyle is not for the faint of heart. It is impossible to tiptoe your way to abundant life or to waltz your way through it. It takes gut-wrenching, sweat-producing, lifestyle-cramping diligence to live a life that is only divinely possible. You must stir up every single ounce of Christian backbone you are able to muster and then cry out to the Holy Spirit for more of His life-enriching power. You must resolve you will never, never, never give up pursuing the heart and plan of God for your singular life.

"Applying all diligence" means you are willing to lavishly pour out everything it takes for you to live a noble life and

an extraordinary life. Mediocre, C+ living is not an option for those who have settled the issue that they will never be content with anything less than the loveliest and most splendid of all lives. One mistake many believers make is that there is certainly an initial and exuberant enthusiasm to receiving Christ, but, often, sadly it is followed by years and years of inertia and vanilla-laced decisions.

God has gifted you with non-refundable, irrevocable, magnificent, and precious promises; He has provided His divine power for everything you will ever possibly need. God has called you to the inexpressible delight of knowing Him intimately and this knowledge will multiply peace and grace to you. Now comes your part: you must work hard at it, you must sweat at it, and you will certainly die to self over it. If you are not willing to do those things, you will never tap into all God has for you this side of Heaven.

The very first and most important place to apply all diligence is in your faith. Faith is the ultimate conviction that what Jesus said is true and because of that conviction, we are able to commit ourselves to His promises and to launch ourselves from the platform He commands. The word that Peter and the Holy Spirit use for faith in this particular phrase is the Greek word *pistis*, which means a holy fervor and strong conviction. When a person believes in something strongly enough, or has decided faith in something, action will always follow belief. Faith is not merely something you will hold in your heart, but it is something that causes you to step out on it and make a difference. The Holy Spirit also used the voice of James to address this issue, which compels believers, at every time in history, to cease being lackadaisical, uninterested Christians, *"Even so faith, if it has no works, is dead, being by itself"* (James 2:17).

What James, Peter, and the Holy Spirit all agree on is faith is more than a heart attitude or a moral compass; faith eternally propels and compels the believer to action and response. Your faith is meant to be followed with a radical response.

Often we have allowed the inconvenience of difficult circumstances to mellow our faith and to make it less than it was in its enthusiastic, infant stages. One way to fight against this deterioration of a vibrant faith is to follow up your faith with the action that ripens and develops it. Faith, at its finest and truest, is not defined by the premise that God will give you what you want, but faith is the confident knowing that God will always do the right thing because He is infinitely and unshakably good.

It is of utmost importance that every believer determines in his or her heart to build their faith daily and not allow it to become stagnate at its core. This diligent determination includes finding delight in reading the Word of God on a daily basis. It might also encompass having a mentor to disciple, lead, and guide. Diligent determination to fan the flame of faith always incorporates the choice to worship in spite of circumstances and not merely because of circumstances. Scripture memorization is one of the most powerful building tools when it comes to the stability and strength of one's faith. A vital and energetic faith is built by solid Bible teaching and the choice to serve in a local Body of believers. All of these practices, and many others, are known as "working diligently" to build your faith.

" ... work out your salvation with fear and trembling; for it is God who is at work in you, both to will and to work for His good pleasure. Do all things without grumbling or disputing" (Philippians 2:12-14).

Being a Christian is not merely asking Jesus Christ into your heart. That is certainly where it eternity begins, but never forget that Christianity is not a one-time experience. The discipline of following Christ, loving Christ, and obeying Christ take a lifetime of lively diligence. Your faith deserves no less than your wholehearted effort every day of every week of every month of every year.

The Reality Check of Peter

After the call for die-hard diligence and the genuine premise that it all begins in our faith, Peter then begins his list, which will take us on a victory march toward a definite objective. Once you have committed to lavishly pouring out every ounce of energy of your life in order to build your faith, it is now time to commence the grunt work. Peter writes this list with much the same tone with which an army general would speak to his troops in order to attain a certain type of advancement or goal. As you advance toward the goal of embracing the life of God's dream for you, march well, march strong, and be motivated by your faith.

Just Do It!

"Now for this very reason, also, applying all diligence, in your faith supply moral excellence..."

The first attribute, after our faith, that Peter commands diligence concerning is moral excellence. Embracing moral excellence does not imply merely being good for goodness sake, but it is a call to model your life after the life of Christ. Your character and your moral choices should always spring from your faith, at which you are working diligently. When you are diligent to demonstrate your faith, it will show through your character choices and will shout through your moral choices. If you find yourself in a place of struggling with morality, with virtue, or with character issues, go back to the basic issue, which will always be your sincere faith.

Some people just seem to be naturally good all the time, don't they? These practically perfect people never say an unkind word, they never seem to compromise either morally or ethically, and are perpetually on their best behavior. Some of us, however, seem always to struggle with character traits and issues that have to do with morality. Some of us are always asking ourselves, and God, questions like these:

- Why did I say that?
- Why did I do that?
- What was I thinking?
- Why didn't I think first?
- Was I even thinking?
- Why do I enjoy that television show?
- Why do I love those kinds of books and magazines?
- Why did I spend perfectly good money to see that movie?

Our faith should always propel us to live a life of moral excellence otherwise it is merely religion. Faith was always meant to go from your head to your heart and make a resounding life difference in that place. A religious spirit attempts to keep your belief system locked in your head and to separate your beliefs from the issues of your heart by thousands of emotional and mental miles.

"If you love Me, you will keep My commandments"
(John 14:15).

Obedience and moral excellence are truly, at their very foundation, a reflection of a believer's love for Jesus. Moral excellence is the visible evidence that I am absolutely head over heels in love with Jesus. Moral excellence was never meant to be a legalistic attempt to please the God who is known as "Holy," but it is a delightful demonstration of heartfelt obedience. Moral excellence at its finest is a respectful imitation of all He embodies and it is my humble attempt that my life would forever be a show and tell of the principles found in His Word.

I love Him therefore when He says it ... I do it!

Getting to Know Him

" ... and in your moral excellence, knowledge ..."

The knowledge Peter is referring to in this passage of Scripture is so much more than just knowing academically who God is. The knowledge Peter and the Holy Spirit are promoting is the type of knowledge that leads to wisdom and discernment and then enables believers to live godly lives.

When my children were young, every time they were leaving the house and the eye of my watchful care, I would empathically remind them, "Use wisdom!" We had trained all five of our children that wisdom is thinking like God thinks. When you know God, your intimate knowledge of Him will invade even your thinking processes and you will begin to tap into His way of thinking. It is vital that a believer assesses every decision and turning point in life by asking themselves a few revealing questions:

: Why am I doing this?

: Would God do this?

: Would God approve of this?

This type of brutal self-examination is what Peter is referring to when he calls believers of every millennia to diligently add knowledge to their faith and also to moral excellence. This is knowledge of the very best, life-changing kind.

If you have found yourself lacking this type of God-approved thinking, there are two practical assignments that you wmight consider:

1 - Ask for wisdom. Ask God to inject your central thinking system with His thoughts, His insight, and His knowledge. In the New Testament book that James, the brother of Jesus wrote, he reminds us, *"But if any of you lacks wisdom, let him ask of God, who gives to all generously and without reproach, and it will be given to him"* (James 1:5).

If you lack ... ask for wisdom. If you find yourself making stupid, foolish decisions ... ask for wisdom. If you don't know what to do ... ask for wisdom.

God never reprimands one of His children who comes to Him in need of more of His knowledge and wisdom. Of course we need His way of thinking ... we are humans and He is God!

2 - Read the Book of Proverbs over and over and over again until your soul and your spirit have embraced the principles and practical application found in this book of Heaven's wisdom. There are thirty-one chapters in Proverbs, which equals one for every day of the month. As you allow the wisdom and prudence the Holy Spirit has revealed through Proverbs to penetrate the foundation of your mind and your decision-making acumen, you will also discover the joy of living a life of wisdom and knowledge.

Just Say No!

" ... and in your knowledge, self-control ..."

Self-control is the ability to get a grip on oneself. Self-control is realizing that being a Christian is not a reckless free-for-all, but neither is it a tightrope where one wrong step can throw you forever into the bottomless abyss.

As we continue on this profitable march with Peter and the Holy Spirit toward the goal of living an abundant and meaningful life this side of Heaven, it is important to note the exact process to which we are called. First, a believer builds up the foundation of faith; then the next step is choosing to live as Christ calls His followers to live. The next purposeful step is using wisdom which is thinking the thoughts of God and that is followed by controlling one's passions.

I have always believed that self-control is not self-control at all but that self-control actually happens when self allows God to be in control and have the final word in everything.

- Should I eat this, Lord?
- Should I buy this, Lord?
- Should I say this, Lord?
- Should I do this, Lord?
- Should I think this, Lord?

There are an abundance of books on the best-seller list that talk about self-fulfillment, self-satisfaction, self-actualization, and self-awareness. However, there are not many books on any list that are bold enough to tackle the virtue of self-control.

Self-control will always become God-control when a person is honest enough to take a lingering look at their strengths and weaknesses. Self-control will always become God-control when a person is courageous enough to spend time on his or her knees asking God to make them strong where they are currently weak. Because these issues of self-control generally have to do with shoring up the glaring weaknesses in our lives, I have found that it generally takes more than one time on my knees. Paul reminds us, in 1 Corinthians 15:31, that the dying to self is to take place daily.

One of the most powerful secrets in allowing God to control the weak areas of your life is to take the time to build up the strength of your spirit. The spirit must be hearty and robust in order to effectively combat the opinion and tantrums of the flesh. Your flesh has powerful appetites and screams the loudest when it does not get its own way.

God-control is a long, steady course of prayer, worship, and the Word of God, which will enable you to learn attitudes that do not come naturally. God-control at its finest and strongest will always channel natural appetites toward God's highest purposes for your life.

If you are struggling in this area of God-control, find an accountant of the faith. Ask a close friend who is a believer to pray for you and with you concerning the areas of struggle in your life. Sometimes, as we march up the mountain of God-control, the value of friendship is what ushers in the victory.

Never, Never, Never Give Up!

" ... and in your self-control, perseverance ..."

Peter instructs everyone who desires the life God has planned during their tenure on Earth that after self-control what is needed is sweaty perseverance. Perseverance is the ability to steadfastly endure suffering or evil without giving up one's faith. The devil's dastardly plan in sending suffering or evil your way is to get you to give up on our faith and to surrender your joy.

The choice is in your hands; will you give up your faith when life is hard?

Will you give in to discouragement, depression, and despair when you don't get your way?

Or, will you dig in your heels, lift your hands in worship, and keep your eyes on Jesus when life is hard?

The best translation of the word "perseverance" is found in the English word, "steadfastness."

Are you steadfast in your faith?

Steadfast believers voluntarily and daily are willing to suffer through difficult events and circumstances for the sake of honor and usefulness. Peter is calling your name across the ages and challenging you to a life of joyful perseverance and to embrace a faith that is steadfast. You will tap into the treasure of that which is life indeed when you dig your heels in both emotionally and spiritually and then determine to fix your eyes only on Jesus.

A steadfast believer looks not at the worst moment of life as a defeat or as an experience that robs from them, but as the opportunity for ultimate and resounding victory. A persevering

Christian views difficult events as experiences that will ultimately and eternally enhance their life and thus their faith. Perseverance is more, so much more, than simply hanging in there by the skin of your teeth. Perseverance is boldly standing firm with joy, purpose, and resolve.

Multi-tasking

" ... and in your perseverance, godliness ..."

And now Peter and the Holy Spirit, challenge us to live a life of godliness in addition to diligence, faith, moral excellence, knowledge, self-control, and perseverance. Godliness is a word that is very difficult to translate from the Greek to the English by merely using one word.

Godliness is the Greek word *eusebia,* which means to look in two different directions. If you are diligently committed to eusebia, you will worship God wholeheartedly and give Him His rightful place in your life and also you will serve your fellow man by being kind, good, and generous. This wonderful Greek word implies your religion has gone from your head to your heart and it has made a beautiful difference in the way you treat people. It means not only are you heavenly minded, but you are also of some earthly good! Because you love God wholeheartedly, one of the greatest calls of your life is to be good to the world in which you live. There is an indescribable *joi de vivre* that fills the soul of one who has allowed their faith to spill out of their life and into the lives of others in meaningful and practical ways.

For you to welcome the call of godliness into your life, it might entail some changes in your daily prayer life.

> During your prayer time, ask God to give you
> divine appointments.
>
> Ask God to "set you up" with people who
> need a friend or need practical help.
>
> Ask God to give you creative ideas on exactly how
> to love those around you, especially those whom it is
> difficult to love.

When you love Jesus, He makes it a joy to love others so work daily at it. A delicious aspect of the abundant life He has provided for us is the call to fill the lives of others with His heart and His hope.

Time for Intensity

" ... and in your godliness, brotherly kindness ..."

When Peter, who has heard from the Holy Spirit on the matter, strongly reminds believers that in addition to godliness, brotherly kindness must also be added, he is calling all of us to an intensity of love and relationship that is rare in our social, media-driven society. Brotherly kindness is an intense, personal love that moves people from mere friends and acquaintances to family. In order to live a life of vitality and with Heaven's enthusiasm, you must view your personal relationships not as nuisances, but as opportunities to enlarge your family. Diligence in brotherly kindness requires a more than "Hi! How are you?" on Sunday mornings as you race out the back door of your church.

Perhaps you should consider setting aside one night a week to invite people into your home. Remember, this is not a nuisance, but it is part of the life plan of God himself for you to live a life that is overflowing with the vigor of Heaven.

In your life, you should embrace some lonely people.

In your life, you should embrace some difficult people.

In your life, you should get to know others who are just plain different than you are.

If you are wealthy, invite those who are struggling financially into your home. If you are an empty-nester, invite a young mom with toddlers to go out to lunch with you. If you are alone with no family in the area, invite a large, rambunctious family to your home for popcorn, homemade cookies, and a game night. Your life will be richer for it.

A mistake that lonely people often make is expecting others to initiate brotherly kindness and then to wait hollowly at home alone. The Bible says you are the one God has called to work diligently at brotherly kindness.

You plan the play days.

You plan the coffee dates.

You plan the potluck dinners.

You work diligently at brotherly kindness. It is an intrinsic and non-negotiable part of the life of joy and relationship that Jesus desires for you to accommodate. Your life will be more abundant when you decide to care for others.

The Love of a Lifetime

" ... and in your brotherly kindness, love."

And finally, and most importantly, Peter reminds us of the important role that heartfelt, deep, genuine love plays in a life of God's design. The Greek word that Peter uses to describe this love is *agape*, which is the specific type of love God gives to us. Quite simply, we are to love others the way we have been loved by the Father.

*"There abides these three ... faith, hope and love ...
but the greatest of these is love"* (1 Corinthians 13:13).

We agape the people in our lives not because we feel like it or because a person has done something to deserve our love, but simply because God loves us in that unconditional way and we are to imitate God in all that we do, say, and choose. We do not love a person because he or she loves us and always acts in a kind and loving manner, but we love because Christ expects it and instructs it.

⋮ Love because you are diligent.

⋮ Love because He is in you and you are in Him.

Agape love can be revealed in uncountable ways every day of life. It is demonstrated by the words that you speak, the way you spend your time, how generously you lavish your affections, what heart attitudes you have embraced, and by your daily actions. Oftentimes, it is in the area of agape love that the struggle between the plan of the enemy and the higher plan of God becomes most obvious.

The devil is rife with glee and out of his mind with enthusiasm when a believer encounters someone who is difficult to love and the child of God then selfishly responds with human emotion rather than with agape love. The devil cannot wait to see how you will respond to someone who gets on your nerves or is unkind to you. The devil, who is the father of all lies, shouts in grand agreement when we justify our inability to reveal agape love to difficult and contentious people.

I believe God often places thorny, cantankerous, and disagreeable people in our lives simply to bring out the strength of unconditional love in us. God gives His children the opportunity to respond with His kind of love when confronted by irascible specimens of humanity. Perhaps that ornery person with whom you contend daily is not meant to reveal your worst side, but to prove to the world, and to the enemy, that you really are like your Dad.

Life on planet Earth is a test and the greatest challenge any believer faces is the test of captious and irritable people. My greatest blessings in life are my relationships with human beings made in the image of God ... and my greatest challenges in life are my relationships with human beings made in the image of God.

Making the unselfish choice to unconditionally love a person does not equal agreeing with their sin, coddling their immaturity, enabling sinful addictions, nor enduring their abuse. There comes a moment in many relationships when the most loving words you can speak to a person are, "Friend ... you need to change! I love you just the way you are ... Jesus loves you just the way you are. But for us to cultivate a healthy relationship that honors God you need to live a godly life."

How to confront sinful choices with those we love is a delicate, often tricky issue and weakens the fiber of many, many relationships. When God values a believer enough to allow a dysfunctional person into his or her personal world, it is of vital importance that the believer presses into God in order to discern exactly how to love this challenging person. Human love is not enough to change someone's life ... it takes agape. If you have found your world invaded by a difficult person who is unhealthy emotionally, consider the following guidelines to help navigate the stormy waters of this type of relationship:

1) Do not bow or agree with their dysfunction. If they are a bitter person, don't agree with their bitterness or allow their bitterness to become part of your emotional make-up. If they are driven by relentless emotional outrage, do not enter into their emotional ridiculousness. Do not allow their dysfunction to penetrate or impact your identity.

2) Ask God for a word. Ask God to give you a creative strategy of exactly how to love this person. Ask God to

give you a Scripture verse that you can daily apply to your relationship with this person.

3) Love them on your knees. Oftentimes, the most valuable time in relationship with a difficult person will be the time that you spend away from their presence, yet in His presence on your knees.

When you are forced to love a person with sincere agape love, it is in that moment in life when God is giving you the opportunity to love like He loves you. Whenever I am given an opportunity to reveal God's love and heart to an especially difficult person, I am in awe of Who God is and how He loves me unconditionally and relentlessly in spite of my dysfunction.

If you have been given the opportunity to love an irritating and problematic specimen of humanity, remind yourself that although Jesus loved wholeheartedly and never withheld His love, He was also wise enough to give the dysfunctional person a heavenly boundary. *"Neither do I condemn you ... go and sin no more"* (John 8:11).

Quality Control

"For if these qualities are yours and are increasing, they render you neither useless nor unfruitful in the true knowledge of our Lord Jesus Christ" (2 Peter 1:8).

You need to own the character traits and spiritual attributes of diligence, faith, moral excellence, knowledge, self-control, perseverance, godliness, brotherly kindness, and love. Not only do you need to claim them as your very own, but their presence in your life should always be on the rise and be maximized. A day should not go by when you have less agape than you did yesterday; with every new day that dawns these extraordinary and miraculous virtues should be more evident in your life and more abundant than they were yesterday. The character of God, revealed through your life, should be perpetually spilling onto all of the people in your world.

Your goal, in embracing an extravagant life this side of Heaven, is to be a fruitful Christian. Peter has just instructed you how to experience great abundance and lavish fruitfulness in your life. For you to live a life void of barrenness and futility, you must apply the coaching of Peter and of the Holy Spirit to your life ... they got it right! The fruitfulness of your life will feed many, many souls including your own.

Short-sighted Amnesia

"For he who lacks these qualities is blind or short-sighted, having forgotten his purification from his former sins" (2 Peter 1:9).

If you are not exhibiting diligence, faith, moral excellence, wisdom, God-control, endurance, Christ-like responses, brotherly kindness, and God's love toward one another, you do not see well. You will quickly need a new pair of spiritual eyeglasses. If you refuse to acknowledge your need to embrace the virtues listed in this passage of life-changing and life-empowering Scripture, you will go through life blindly, always groping for direction and for purpose. The aforementioned list of biblical attributes is your guiding purpose in life and will give you clear directions for the life of God's dreams. If you continuously refuse to choose death to your flesh and to submit your will to His greater plan, you will be guilty of making life-determining decisions based upon short-term feelings and not the long haul of His calling.

If you continue to drudge through life on your strength, warped by emotional and weak choices, you have forgotten that you were a sinner in need of agape love and kindness. The phrase in this verse, *"blind or short-sighted"* actually means closing your eyes to what is true. Open your eyes to the truth, and diligently pursue the life God has called you to on Earth.

A Stumble-free Life

"Therefore, brethren, be all the more diligent to make
certain about His calling and choosing you; for as long
as you practice these things, you will never stumble"
(2 Peter 1:10).

No one enjoys falling down and scraping a knee, breaking a leg, or doing internal damage. You really don't want to stumble spiritually! God has chosen and called you to walk with health and strength and the only way that is possible is to obey the Word of God. The only guarantee that you will never stub your toe or do severe damage to your life is when you diligently choose to entwine your life with the virtues of God.

The Olympics have long held a magnetic fascination for me. How I love watching the sleek bodies of swimmers who have given their lives to mastering the speed of cutting through the water. I am glued to the television set every four years watching skaters, gymnasts, and divers who have ultimate control over every sinew and muscle in their disciplined bodies. But my favorite event of all to watch is one of Olympic greatness and prowess that seems Herculean in effort: I am hypnotized by the men and women who run the 26.2-mile marathon.

Hundreds upon hundreds of runners, from every nation in the world, line up with breathless anticipation at the starting line of this unmatchable race. Each athlete has a dream in his or her heart to run with strength and diligence and to cross the eventual finish line if not first, then at least with honor. The judge places the microphone to his lips and shouts, "On your mark ... get set ... Go!" And with that two-letter word, comes the blast of the gun that marks the beginning of the race for all who have determined to run. Every runner has his or her eyes set on the eventual goal and most have trained for years for this one life-defining moment.

And yet, in spite of years of training, in spite of vitamins, expensive running shoes, and in spite of trim, athletic bodies, not everyone finishes well. Some stumble and fall just yards or even inches from the finish line. When my couch potato body sees that poor fella or gal lose their footing just seconds away from the "Well done!" my heart meets the girth of my belly and I am sick for the runner.

How will you finish your race? If you are diligent to put into daily practice this list of God-charged character traits, you will finish well and you will finish strong. You will not stumble nor fall. You will finish the course of your life with no regrets and will have experienced an extraordinary life of Heaven-delivered abundance and growth.

Your Grand Entrance

"For in this way the entrance into the eternal kingdom of our Lord and Savior Jesus Christ will be abundantly supplied to you" (2 Peter 1:11).

Kingdom living at its best is always attained when obedience is honored. Virtuous living is not merely a list of good and bad ... right and wrong ... yes and no ... but it is the acknowledgement and the agreement that God's ways are always best. Neither you nor I nor any other created being has ever had a better idea than God. Your life will be a rare and beautiful reflection of the beauty and joy of God's character when you obey with diligence the life that the Scripture presents.

Ruth's Grand Entrance

Ruth Bell Graham went to be with the Lord just after turning eighty-seven years old in June of 2007. Growing up in war-torn China had toughened her to life's hard edges, but it did not make her callous or hard. Ruth somehow developed a zest for life and a love for God that few of us have chosen to embrace this side of eternity. Her dedication to the Word of God and to the diligence of obedience is her legacy. Ruth discovered a secret of abundant living that you and I sometimes ignore: Ruth had an undying faith in Jesus and diligently pursued a life of highest obedience. On Ruth's tombstone are written these words:

"End of Construction ... Thank you for your patience!"

Prayer for Life

"Lord Jesus, I love You so much. I embrace the principles found in the Word of God and I ask that You will give me the strength to daily walk out the game plan found in 2 Peter 1:2-11. I pray You will find me diligent in my faith and when my time on Earth is done, You will welcome me into Your presence with a resounding, 'Well done!' In the name of Jesus I pray, Amen."

Declaration for Life

"I declare that I will embrace a diligent faith and choose to be morally excellent in all of my decisions. I declare that I will get to know God better every day of my life and that I will ask Him to control my fleshly urges. I declare that I will persevere in godliness, brotherly kindness, and in love."

Scripture for Life

Now for this very reason also, applying all diligence, in your faith supply moral excellence, and in your moral excellence, knowledge, and in your knowledge, self-control, and in your self-control, perseverance, and in your perseverance, godliness, and in your godliness, brotherly kindness, and in your brotherly kindness, love (2 Peter 1:5-7).

Words of Life

"Down through the years I turned to the Bible and found in it all that I needed." — *Ruth Bell Graham*

CHAPTER 6

The Thrill of a Defiant Life!

WHEN Darlene Rose was a mere ten years old, a missionary came to her church in Ames, Iowa, and after delivering a stirring sermon, gave an altar call to the teens and college age students, begging them to give their lives to foreign missions. Darlene was sitting on the back row during the altar call and felt a firm but loving hand on her shoulder. However, when she looked around no one was there. Darlene focused her heart and attention once again on the fervent missionary who was imploring young people to give their lives to missionary service but this time could not ignore the voice that she heard audibly behind her, "Would you go anywhere for me no matter what the cost?"

Darlene Rose, although only one decade old, walked bravely to the front and gave her life for service in the Kingdom of God. She was the only one who responded that winter night.

After marrying Russell Diebler, a veteran missionary in August of 1937, Darlene and Russell landed in Batavia, Java, on August 18, 1938, their first wedding anniversary. They had been married only a little more than four years when Pearl Harbor was attacked and within two months, Darlene and Russell were taken as prisoners of war.

The Dieblers were taken into the mountains by their captors on March 13, 1942, where all of the men in their group were viciously beaten. The Japanese then came to take the bruised and battered men to a different location. As Darlene's young, injured husband was loaded into the back of the enemy's truck, he said to her, "Remember one thing, dear. God said He would never leave us or forsake us." Darlene never saw her husband on Earth again.

Darlene recalls that as the vehicle pulled away from the

weakened group of women and children, she experienced complete peace because she believed Romans 8:28 means exactly what it says it means.

"And we know that God causes all things to work together for good to those who love God, to those who are called according to His purpose."

Darlene knew, in the deepest caverns of her heart, that her mighty God would work even this tragedy together for His highest good.

During the next three years of being imprisoned by the Japanese, Darlene and her fellow missionaries who had also been taken captive, were forced to eat dogs and rats to stay alive. They were imprisoned in shacks on the side of a remote mountain and knew that without a miracle they would never be rescued.

One night during this awful time, Darlene heard a noise and went out into the hallway of the ramshackle building. There she saw a man who had on a black sarong and was holding a machete in his hand. She recognized him immediately as one of the Bogus people who were pirates and savage murderers. Darlene was a petite woman in her early twenties, but was well acquainted with the power and strength that comes not from human resources, but from the Holy Spirit. She chased this daunting enemy out of her home and down the roadway. On the mountain trail, this particular night, was an entire gang of Bogus men who had been marauding the captive's homes and raping the women there. When these enemies of the people of God saw her, they ran in fear of their lives down the mountain trail. As Darlene walked wearily, yet gratefully, back to her primitive home that night, she quoted the Scripture, *"The angel of the Lord encamps around those who fear Him, and rescues them"* (Psalm 34:7).

Night after night the Bogus pirates came back to the village, but they only stood outside the shack in which Darlene lived and never entered it again.

Years later, when Darlene returned to New Guinea as a missionary after World War II, she met a young man who had been part of the Bogus gang during the war. This handsome young man was now a Christian and served the Jesus of the gospels. When Darlene asked him why the Bogus pirates had never again attacked her home, but only stood outside and looked at it, he replied, "Because of all of those people in white who stood guard around your house night after night after night."

The Power of the Unseen

"Now faith is the assurance of things hoped for, the conviction of things not seen. For by it the men of old gained approval. By faith we understand that the worlds were prepared by the word of God so that what is seen was not made out of things which are visible" (Hebrews 11:1-3).

God wants you to know that just because you can't see it ... doesn't mean that He won't do it! What God desires to do in us and through us simply begins with a word that is dropped into our spirits from a teaching or during a daily quiet time. God may whisper a possibility into your heart during a great worship service or while you are meditating on a Christian devotional book. It is in these types of moments that you are given the gift of something invisible from God; it is something unseen but it is real, nonetheless, and it then begins to take root in your heart. God is delighted to place the unfertilized seed of an idea ... a possibility ... a dream ... into the heart of one of His children and then He waits.

I believe God loves the gift of time. God knows that all things, which eventually become great in our human sphere, will germinate and flourish during the pressure that only time can furnish. A piece of coal is black and flakey, until put under extreme pressure. When time and pressure combine for a miraculous effect in a piece of inexpensive coal, a diamond is the result. The longer that the diamond stays under pressure is seen in the glory and color of the many facets that are formed.

So it is with you and the piece of coal God has given you. You know this piece of coal is from God because every time you pray, it is there. In conversations not of your own making, the possibility is presented. You dream about your piece of coal; it is your first new thought in the morning and your last weary thought at night. You dream about the piece of coal God has revealed to you and are desperate for time and pressure to do its completed work.

Even though you can't see the coal, the diamond, or the process ... you know it. You just know it!

Everything that is a current tangible was conceived as an intangible; everything that today is visibly seen was birthed in the unseen. Everything that today is a visible component of your life took its first baby breath as the invisible. Everything that is worth spending your life on and giving every waking breath for was forged as an invisible dream, an intangible word, and as an unseen, yet vital, prayer. Just because you don't see something in reality today does not mean you won't get it or that it will not happen tomorrow. Just because you don't see something in reality today does not mean God won't do it. God specializes in the unseen, yet promised. He delights in the invisible, yet genuine. God is focused on the call of your life toward His Kingdom of faith. This is an extraordinary way to do life!

When you receive a troubling doctor's report ... you rejoice.

When your marriage is crumbling ... you stand in prayer and in faith.

When your child has turned his or her back on God ... you worship.

When the bills are bigger than your income ... you give, and give again.

When the unkindness of a family member penetrates your soul ... you reach out in agape love.

We are a people who build our lives on the strong foundation of that which we do not see in the natural. We construct an abundant life on the invisible and unshakable goodness of God. We create a life of rich and rare resources on the faithfulness of God. We marvel not at what we are able to do, but on what He is able to do through us. We are more aware of the blessings of God than we are of the ground upon which we walk.

If you long for more than an ordinary and comfortable life, then you will be more aware of God's unseen presence and outrageous kindness than you are of your loud, demanding, and mountainous circumstances. When God places a word of hope or faith in the spirit of a human being concerning their impossible circumstances, He seals it with the promise of His Word. When God gives you a dream, ask Him for the accompanying Scripture to seal it. God's Word always prepares the way for the miraculous during our tenure on Earth. What you see with your eyes is the untruth, and what is viewed only with your eyes of faith is the ultimate and resounding truth. The time between when you receive your unseen yet audible word from God and when this word comes to visibility is called the testing of your faith. What does a believer do during this time of testing?

Worship in Spite of

"By faith Abel offered to God a better sacrifice than Cain, through which he obtained the testimony that he was righteous, God testifying about his gifts, and through faith, though he is dead, he still speaks"
(Hebrews 11:4).

Faith will always call a steadfast believer to worship and to offer the glorious sacrifice of praise. Worship is offered in faith regardless of how a believer feels or what he sees with his natural eyes. Worship is never dependent upon answered prayer, emotional response, or happy days, but it is a dynamic response to who He is. If you refuse to worship based upon your circumstances in life, you will never know the joy and fulfillment of living by faith. If you balk rather than worship, you will never see the unseen. Making a deliberate and defiant choice to worship rather than panic is truly the primary evidence of faith. We worship a God whom we are not able to see with our eyes but know intimately and completely in our hearts.

If you doubt God is good, you will never be able to worship Him. If your intensive desire is to live beyond the dash of your life, then you will leave a rich and long-lasting legacy of worship. This is what the heroes and heroines of the faith do in every generation: they break out into an unrelenting song at the most difficult moment of their lives. Defiantly joyful Christians refuse to allow the song in their hearts to die no matter what they see with their natural eyes. Because we don't worship our circumstances, frankly, it does not matter how difficult or heartbreaking our circumstances become. The song goes on ... and on and on and on. We know that we worship a God who never changes and so the song of our faith grows louder and stronger while the storm of our circumstances rage.

Walk and Worship

*"By faith Enoch was taken up so that he would
not see death; and he was not found because God
took him up; for he obtained the witness that
before his being taken up he was pleasing to God"*
(Hebrews 11:5).

Enoch is listed in the Bible's Hall of Fame of Faith. His name
is up there with Noah, Abraham, and Moses. Enoch did not part
the Red Sea or save all of humanity in a boat he had built. Enoch
did not stand in faith for a baby when he was one hundred years
old. All Enoch did was walk with God. And yet, walking with God
was enough to certify his inclusion in the greatest list of believers
that has ever been written. If it was good enough for Enoch, my
guess is it will be good enough for you as well. There is delight,
strength, and virtue in simply walking with God.

*Enoch lived sixty-five years, and became the
father of Methuselah. Then Enoch walked with
God three hundred years after he became the
father of Methuselah, and he had other sons and
daughters. So all the days of Enoch were three
hundred and sixty-five years. Enoch walked with God;
and he was not, for God took him.* (Genesis 5:21-24)

These four verses from the fifth chapter of Genesis are amazing
in every way; twice the length of Enoch's life is mentioned and
twice the Holy Spirit records that *"Enoch walked with God."*
This is evidence that what it takes to genuinely please God is just
the fact you have chosen to walk with Him.

The word *walk* that is used to describe Enoch's intimate
relationship with God means much more than to accompany God
down the road of life. The meanings of this word walk are rich
and varied in texture and among their intriguing definitions are:

to worship God, to be intimate with God, to pursue God, and to imitate God.

Walking with God always means worshiping God. You will never walk in God's destiny for your life until you are willing to worship Him every day in every circumstance. It takes my breath away the moment I realize that only friends walk together. Friendship with God embraces the walk of worship. It is what Enoch did and you can do it, too. Walking with God in friendship and in intimacy becomes a definite possibility when you have chosen to worship in spite of and not simply because of.

Get to Work!

"By faith Noah, being warned by God about things not yet seen, in reverence prepared an ark for the salvation of his household, by which he condemned the world, and became an heir of the righteousness which is according to faith" (Hebrews 11:7).

Noah obeyed the voice of God and built an ark according to God's specific and complete instructions. This was a work of great fortitude and loneliness, and yet Noah continued in the legacy of the specific call God had for him and his family. However, Noah did not begin his life by working for God; he first worshiped God and then he walked with God. Noah was actually chosen to do this enormous job at this historical crossroads because of the way he had conducted his life.

Never buy into the western deception that working for God is more vital than your worship or your walk. The truth is your choice to worship and the intimacy of your walk prepare you for the great work God has for your life. You will never do all God has called you to do without first being committed to worship and to the joy of the walk. If you don't place primary value on worship and walking with God, your work for Him will be a frustrating drain of the purpose of your life.

Noah built a colossal ship in the middle of dry Earth. God had warned Noah about something he could not see with his human eyes. It was a warning of something that had never happened prior to Noah's life and it has not ever happened again. Noah had no historical precedent upon which to build his boat; He only had the word of the Lord. If God has called you to do something immense, do not look to history for perceived precedence. If you have truly heard the voice of God like Noah did, chances are that it has never actually been done before.

God's word for your life is a unique frontier that probably no one has ever before pioneered. It's your and yours alone. Listen to God's particular word for your life. Worship Him loudly regardless of what you see in the natural. Walk with Him in friendship and in intimacy. And then ... you get to work for Him.

Noah acted upon the word that was given to him by God and the fantastic result was that his entire family was saved. If your heart's desire is for your family to be saved and to make a significant difference in the lives of those around you, learn from Abel, Enoch, and Noah. Listen to the Word of the Lord, find delight in worshiping Him and not in your circumstances, and then obey Him even when it does not make one bit of sense. We are called believers because we believe in what we do not see!

Outside or Inside?

Did you notice that we skipped a verse in this string of Scriptures we are studying? It was neglected on purpose so we could wring out the meaning of this message as an emphatic point of exclamation.

"And without faith it is impossible to please Him,
for he who comes to God must believe that He is
and that He is a rewarder of those who seek Him"
(Hebrews 11:6).

When we defiantly live outside the parameters of faith it is impossible to experience the pleasure of God. There is no way to underestimate the importance of corralling your thought life, your words, and your choices to live vitally within the boundaries of believing that God exists and He rewards those who choose to walk with Him. The choice to live inside of faith or outside of faith is the singular most important choice any human being will ever make. The choice is yours daily.

I know faith is a real place because I live there. Although I can't see it with my fifty-something -year-old sparkling blue eyes, I know faith has borders. Just as I can sleep inside my house any given night and enjoy the comfort and protection of brick walls, a solid foundation, and roof with a twenty year warrantee, or choose to pitch a tent and camp outside in the wilderness where wild animals roam and the elements invade, I can also either live inside of or outside of faith in God. God wants you to be located at the address of faith in Him. If you have chosen to live outside the parameters of glorious faith, it will be impossible to please Him.

Hebrews 11 is the Hall of Fame of the Faithful of God. It is the account of those who chose to live in faith ... by faith ... and through faith. Every individual, male and female, rich and poor, educated or not, married or single, barren or fruitful, must make this same decision. You will not make it through life without being confronted many, many times about whether or not you will stay at your address of faith. Hebrews 11 honors men and women who lived at the address of faith and received a word from God for their lives at their specific time in history. And although faced with horrific circumstances and events, they held on tightly to their mandate from command central in Heaven. They did not let go of their faith regardless of what they confronted in the natural.

Post-menopausal Mama

*"By faith even Sarah herself received ability to
conceive, even beyond the proper time of life, since
she considered Him faithful who had promised"*
(Hebrews 11:11).

Never make the mistake that you are the only person in all
of created history who has faced impossible circumstances. Sarah
went through menopause before she conceived a baby! Now
that is what the medical community would label "impossible"
and "ridiculous." Sarah was an old, shriveled-up woman who in
the natural had no reason to believe she would ever give birth
to a bouncing baby boy. But God spoke to Sarah and her husband
when they were well past the age of changing diapers, of getting
up in the middle of the night to feed a wailing baby, and of potty
training a toddler. God was not limited by the demise of her
reproductive system. Because Sarah *considered Him faithful who
had promised*, there are now millions and millions of people in
the Jewish nation.

What seems impossible in the natural is not even a speed
bump to God. When the angel said to Mary, *"For nothing
will be impossible with God"* (Luke 1:37), he meant it. God
specializes in the impossible ... it is what He does best. You honor
God when you stand at the address of faith and look down the
road for the impossible to become possible.

Sarah did not focus on her unproductive womb, the ancient
date on her birth certificate, or on the futility and improbability
of her circumstances, but wrapped her heart and mind around the
God who had promised a baby.

The Eternal Power of Ending Well

"By faith Jacob, as he was dying, blessed each of the sons of Joseph, and worshiped, leaning on the top of his staff" (Hebrews 11:21).

How does a man worship when his life on Earth is over? Is it possible to leave Earth with no regrets, no remorse, and no desire to do it all again? So many people ache for one more day of living and just one more hour to enjoy their human existence. Jacob was able to worship while he was dying because he was not gazing on all the beauty he was leaving, but at the invisible world where he was going.

The true test of a man or a woman's faith is how they end their days in the world this side of Heaven. You can either lock into bitterness and the unfairness of circumstances or you can bless those you leave behind. When one chooses the address of faith while the storms of life roar, worship is the only lasting legacy worth leaving. Those who finish well choose to bless and determine to worship.

The wonder of dying with grace and with joy leaves the finest legacy one could ever hope to establish. Choosing to bless your family and to worship your God in your final days and hours, will eternally trump houses, lands, and anything else of earthly value you will leave behind. The song of your life will have more impact than the size of your bank account when your feet are no longer on terra firma.

Jacob chose to bless and worship! We are all given the eternal privilege of choosing how we will spend the last, precious moments of life ... what will you choose?

"By faith Joseph, when he was dying, made mention of the exodus of the sons of Israel, and gave orders concerning his bones" (Hebrews 11:22).

Joseph, the man who was beaten by his brothers, sold into slavery, accused of sexual harassment, and spent years in an Egyptian prison, demonstrated no regret or bitterness in his final hours. Instead, Joseph chose to prophesy while he was dying. Because Joseph was more aware of the presence of God than he was of his temporary yet terrible circumstances, Joseph had the faith to look into the future and gaze at the goodness of God being spilled out upon the people of God. Joseph did not die a bitter old man filled with blame and anger, but in his dying moments he talked about the promises of God being fulfilled in the nation of Israel.

Joseph chose to prophesy. We are all given the eternal privilege of choosing how we will spend the last, precious moments of life ... what will you choose?

The Palace was not Good Enough

"By faith Moses, when he had grown up, refused to
be called the son of Pharaoh's daughter, choosing
rather to endure ill-treatment with the people of
God than to enjoy the passing pleasures of sin"
(Hebrews 11:24-25).

A man who chose a life in the desert herding his father-in-law's sheep rather than the food, extravagance, and opulence of the palace should have his head examined. But Moses was an extraordinary man whose eyesight was not blinded by the luxury of creature comforts.

It is a feat of spiritual strength and tenacity to choose the Kingdom of God when your life is falling apart, but to choose to serve God when your life is at an all time high is another arena of faith altogether. Moses chose a challenging and difficult life with the people of God rather than the soft and extravagant life in the palace because he saw something better in faith. Could there be anything better than life in the palace? Apparently Moses believed so. What do you believe?

We are just so human sometimes, aren't we? We tend to be fooled and trapped by the aura of success and palace living. Think again. Discern again. Choose again.

The Shout of Faith!

"By faith the walls of Jericho fell down after they had been encircled for seven days" (Hebrews 11:30).

While the army of God marched around Jericho, they were not consumed by the size of the city or by the multitude of the enemy troops, but they were amazed at the size of the army of angels who had gathered for the victory shout. These wilderness-weary people of God obeyed the word they had heard and knew there would come that victory moment when the shout of faith would change everything!

When you are weary because of years spent in the wilderness, hunker down into the presence of God and hear His voice. Intently obey His given strategy and when the time comes ... shout with every fiber of your being. In that moment, you will hear the host of Heaven join their voices in a victory roar at the faith of your life. The shout of faith changes everything. Choose to shout.

What are You Looking at?

The devil is intent on deceiving the people of God to buy into the lie that the only thing in life that really matters is what we see with our eyes. He will orchestrate situations to discourage your diligence and to weaken your stand in faith. You must determine that nothing else is worthy of your focus or attention but God and God alone. While the storms of life blow, and they will, you must be mesmerized by the goodness and the strength of God.

"And without faith it is impossible to please Him, for he who comes to God must believe that He is and that He is a rewarder of those who [diligently] *seek Him"* (Hebrews 11:6).

God rewards people who diligently seek Him regardless of the pleasure or pain of the events they are experiencing. The key to receiving the reward God has for you depends on your level of determination and your willingness to do whatever is necessary to achieve that goal. We all possess the same promises, the same faith, the same power, the same Holy Spirit, and the same Jesus. If you desperately desire the reward of God, then you will diligently seek Him and Him alone. That's it ... that's all ... you have to have faith. You simply must believe He exists and He exists to reward those who seek Him above all else. You must embrace this as an all-consuming lifestyle in which everything else pales in comparison to worshiping Him and walking with Him.

With every breath you take you must place yourself prominently in His presence and rest there. This takes spiritual diligence, the sweat born of tenacity, and the refusal to give up in your pursuit of all that He is.

Not all translations of Hebrews 11:6 have the word *diligently* in the verse, but it is there in the Greek as a reminder of how we seek Him. We must more than simply seek Him ... we must diligently seek Him. This word diligently in the Greek means "one who seeks something so passionately and determinedly that he literally exhausts all his power in the search." If you take this part of your life assignment with a laid-back, inattentive attitude, you will never go far in the fulfillment of God's call and dream for your life. You must immerse yourself in the singular pursuit of knowing Him during your tenure on Earth.

Diligence is required not only in the Kingdom of God, but is a requirement for any avenue of greatness.

Ask Olympic athletes about diligence ... ask successful

moms about diligence ... ask award-winning gardeners about diligence ... ask women with immaculate homes about diligence ... ask concert pianists about diligence ... ask research scientists about diligence.

Why should it be any different when it comes to matters of our faith? Living in that place of stubborn faith must not be a minor issue in your life but it must capture your complete and undivided attention every day of your life. The outcome of every other single area of your life will be determined by this one decision—will you be diligent in your faith or not?

The challenge of being diligent in one's faith is scripted in several daily disciplines.

1) Your eyesight: You must see what others do not see.
2) Your embraced beliefs: You must believe what others refuse to believe.
3) Your mouth: You must use your mouth as a tool that breaks through the seen to the unseen. You must confess with your mouth what has not, as yet, been seen in the natural.
4) Be stubborn: Stay insistent in your resolve that will push the powers of hell aside.

No one has ever said that staying in a place of faith is easy, but it is certainly a whole lot more fun to believe!

20-20 Vision

What are you looking at? What has captured your attention? What you choose to see by faith is what you will receive. Refuse the limited eyesight of an unbeliever and choose to have the visionary capacity of Noah, Sarah, Moses, and Jacob. Faith looks at a desert and sees a luscious and vibrant garden springing up in that very place. Faith looks at an overgrown and expansive wilderness and sees a roadway to destiny in its place. Faith looks at nothing and sees everything.

If you only see what you are seeing, you are only living a half-life. It's not so much about seeing the good stuff or the bad stuff, but it is completely about seeing God's stuff!

As I read, time after time, this great faith chapter located in the Book of Hebrews, filled with the testimonies of ordinary people who diligently pursued the promises of God with defiant faith, I am reminded I am not alone. The people whose names are recorded in the eleventh chapter of Hebrews knew the heartless lies of the visible and the sparkling truth of the invisible.

Therefore since we have so great a cloud of witnesses surrounding us, let us also lay aside every encumbrance and the sin which so easily entangles us, and let us run with endurance the race that is set before us, fixing our eyes on Jesus, the author and perfecter of faith, who for the joy set before Him endured the cross, despising the shame, and has sat down at the right hand of the throne of God. For consider Him who has endured such hostility by sinners against Himself, so that you will not grow weary and lose heart. (Hebrews 12:1-3)

If you could only see with the eyes of faith, what you would see are people, heroes and heroines of the faith, piled up around us on every side. And all of these men and women who have gone before us are cheering! They are shouting words of encouragement and believing that you are going to make it ... just like they did.

Do you see them? Or do you only see you? Are you merely aware of your mortal and frustrating existence? The people that are applauding your life are those who from every generation chose to see what they could not see with their natural eyes. The ones who are yelling the loudest and with the greatest gusto are those who withstood the fiercest difficulties of life in order to do the will of God. All of those who have gone before you are standing and watching with grand anticipation the choices you will make as you walk your earthly path. If you listen, you will hear the acclaim and support of the men and women who held fast to the Word of God and ultimately saw His promises come to pass in their lives.

The Reality of the Unseen

Toward the end of World War II, Darlene Rose and her other missionary friends who were held in captivity, began to hear the bombs drop night after night after night. Darlene and the other POWs would gather up lifeless bodies each morning and bury them on the side of the mountain.

One night, during an especially intense bombing of their camp, Darlene had thrown herself down into the safety of a deep ditch. All of the captives had elected a favorite spot they ran to each night during the shower of bombs and Darlene's was this cavity in the earth that had grown increasingly familiar to her. However, this particular night, God spoke to Darlene shortly after she had nestled into her ditch and told her to go back in the house and retrieve a Bible that belonged to one of the other women.

Darlene's Bible had long been confiscated, but as a little girl she had memorized literally hundreds of verses of Scripture. When her cruel captors had confiscated her beloved Bible, in actuality, it did not matter because Darlene knew the joy of hiding God's Word in her heart.

As Darlene raced through the dark night, the bombs came closer and closer to the encampment. She had clearly heard God's voice telling her to go inside their home and rescue the Bible and so she was determined to obey rather than stay in the safety of her ditch. After Darlene found the Bible and hurried back outside, the bombs began to subside and the raid came to an end. Darlene helped others back into the barracks and the next morning, she saw a woman sleeping on the floor rather than on her bed. This woman told Darlene that she had tried to save her mattress during the storm of bombs the night before and had thrown it over the spot where Darlene always hid in the ditch. When the woman had gone back to get it, the mattress had been hit by a bomb. The voice of God, and the Word of God, had saved Darlene Rose's life.

Darlene was only twenty-six years old when the war ended. The Allied soldiers came and rescued the missionary captives and Darlene left on the very last boat. As Darlene's boat pulled away from the shore, she thought to herself, *I will never come back here again. I am going home to America and I will stay there with my family.* But as her ship pulled away from the war-torn shore, the natives whom she and her husband had led to the Lord stood on the shore singing, "God be with you till we meet again!"

In that instant, Darlene knew she would come back to this land of her captivity, and yet the land of her truest destiny. Darlene began to yell from the deck of the boat, with tears streaming down her cheeks, "I will come back! I will come as soon as I can!"

After spending only a few short years in America, Darlene spent forty more years in the jungles of this nation because she had heard God's voice. Darlene obeyed in faith the word God had spoken to her heart as a ten-year-old girl in Iowa. Darlene Rose lived a life of more abundance and joy than you and I can imagine because what she didn't see was more real than what she saw.

Prayer for Life

"Dear Jesus, I love You so much. I pray that You will speak to me clearly and that I will hear Your voice. I pray You will use me to my fullest capacity at this moment in history. I will go anywhere for You. In Jesus' name I pray, Amen."

Declaration for Life

"I declare that I will walk by faith and not by sight. I will worship God, I will walk with God, and I will also work for

God. I refuse to be paralyzed or hypnotized by what I see in the natural, but I will base every decision and every prayer on what I am unable to see with my natural eyes. Just because I do not see it today does not mean that God will not do it."

Scripture for Life

"Now faith is the assurance of things hoped for, the conviction of things not seen ... And without faith it is impossible to please Him for he who comes to God must believe that He is and that He is a rewarder of those who seek Him" (Hebrews 11: 1; 6).

Words of Life

"Lassie, be a good soldier for Jesus Christ." — An older missionary, spoken to Darlene Rose

CHAPTER 7

Gifts That Trump Human Pain

PAULA THOMAS lived across the hall from me during my freshman year in college. We both hailed from the Northeast, and attending a Midwestern Christian university was culture shock for both of us. Neither Paula nor I had ever experienced the delight of cheese grits, country western music, or eighty-degree weather in March prior to attending college in the state where the wind comes sweeping down the plains. I was from New York State, while Paula had been raised in Pennsylvania, and the sisterhood our home states represented was embraced by the two of us during the first few weeks of our freshman year.

Our brother wing invited us to go to an authentic Mexican restaurant one night at the very beginning of the school year. This restaurant had Mexican music blaring through the speakers, all waiters and waitresses were dressed in Mexican attire, and danced their way from table to table. Neither Paula nor I had ever placed a taco, burrito, or enchilada into our mouths before this evening, and we instantly knew our world had been wonderfully enlarged. Paula, however, established a unique reputation for herself that first night under the starry lights at Casa Bonita. She fell in love with the Mexican dessert called *sopapillas,* which were little pieces of fried dough, rolled in cinnamon and sugar. After the corner was ripped off the sopapilla, it was filled with gobs and gobs of honey. Paula, who was a size four soaking wet, ate a grand total of fourteen sopapillas that night!

Paula had lived under an older sister's imposing shadow. Paula's sister was a gorgeous, stately, and talented beauty queen, but I never detected any resentment in Paula's heart toward her sister ... only genuine love and respect.

Paula's roommate, Trudy, was the most fabulous girl on

our floor. Everyone either wanted to be like Trudy or to be Trudy's best friend. When Trudy made the cheerleading squad, although Paula and I did not, Trudy was gracious beyond measure. Trudy met her future husband the first day her foot stepped on campus in the registration lines. He was handsome, athletic, smart, and godly. Neither Paula nor I had a date our entire freshman year.

Paula loved Trudy dearly and delighted in every one of her victories. I never detected any resentment in Paula's heart toward this Heaven-sent roommate, only genuine love and respect.

Paula worked diligently to excel in the classroom and often spearheaded study sessions late into the night. However, the thing I recall most vividly about Paula was her intrinsic and generous kindness. She was kind to everyone regardless of skin color, background, or personality type.

Paula was an avid runner, and I hated every single minute I spent on the university's track trying to earn the dreaded aerobic points. At the end of our freshman year, we were required to run 1.3 miles in under twelve minutes. I had worried about it for weeks and knew I would probably receive an "F" for this end-of-year test. Paula finished well and strong and actually lapped me a couple of times on the indoor track. However, when she crossed the finish line for her final lap, she didn't stop for water but looped around to find me. Paula joined me at my much slower pace, quoting Bible verses, and encouraging me to run harder. Due to Paula's insistence and encouragement, I crossed the much-anticipated finish line at just seconds under the required twelve minutes.

The next year, our sophomore year, Paula developed a precious ministry on our floor. She poured herself into praying for the girls on our floor and encouraging each one through simple acts of kindness and affirmation. We often found little notes or Scripture verses tucked under our pillows at night. When someone had a bad day, it was to Paula they ran for prayer. When any of our girls suffered broken hearts, it was Paula who met them for breakfast and spent time with them. When the stress of college life became too great, it was Paula who would gather the troops, pop popcorn, and mother us all back into stability and joy.

For the final two years of our college life, Paula and I moved to other floors in other dormitories, but continued to enjoy one another's friendship and company for the entire four years at the university. I was honored when she asked me to be in her wedding in October of 1977.

As the years passed, I lost track of Paula, as college friends often do, but I knew she had a son and a daughter and had stayed in the Midwest while I moved around the country with my pastor husband and growing clan of five children.

A few years ago, I noticed through a university publication that she had returned to work at our alma mater and I was thrilled for her and for the university. I am often back on campus in my role as the chaplain on the alumni board of directors and whenever I am there, Paula and I make sure to spend a few minutes together talking, laughing, and often crying.

In the fall of 2011, I could tell that there was something different about Paula ... something indescribably beautiful, but melancholy at the same time. As we stood outside our beloved chapel that September morning, I asked her how her husband, Gary, was doing. She responded by saying he was having a very difficult time dealing with grief. I looked at her blankly, apologized, and then asked, "Did someone die?"

"You didn't know, Carol? Our son drowned this summer."

Pain

Pain is a four-letter word that has the potential to violently erase abundance from any person's life. The pain can be emotional, physical, or mental, but its violence has the potency to devastate the landscape of anyone's life. Pain is able to penetrate the life of a man or a woman in a myriad of ways and forms, but the damage it does to a person's heart is tragically the same regardless of the source. Pain is often delivered through the messenger of health issues, relationship struggles, or career disappointment. Sometimes pain stealthily penetrates the lives of unsuspecting people through loneliness, grief, poor moral choices, or lack of self-esteem. There are moments in the lives of many people when they are not even sure what brought the pain into their life, only that it is agonizingly there. There are also other awful moments in life when a man or woman, in a raw state, may wonder if Jesus is even aware of their singular pain.

Oftentimes pain is of the self-inflicted variety. Due to poor choices, sin, or the mishandling of life's demands, we have become our own worst enemy. This type of pain is doubly painful because it is rife with regret and "if-onlies." Pain is also birthed when the lives of others conspire against us and we find ourselves victimized by their poor choices, sin, or the mishandling of life's demands. Pain also can come straight from the enemy himself and is found horrifically leering down the destiny of our lives. One of the very few things that Satan does well is to stir up pain in the life of a believer.

Although the birthplace of pain is never found in the heart of God, our God is glorious enough and good enough to use pain triumphantly so it bears the end result of fashioning the object of the pain into someone breathtakingly beautiful. God knew that in this fallen world not only would we be forced to suffer momentary pain, but also to endure the latitude of longer pain. God knew, because of the complexity of living on Earth where sin abounds, that His beloved children would be challenged not only to face pain sporadically in life, but also to choose necessary pain for a greater and more eternal good. Therefore, because it is His will that His children would always live in the abundance of life, He, in His marvelous and compassionate mercy, has given gifts to His children which are miraculously accurate in helping to cope with, lessen, and even to destroy the pain involved. God, the loving

Father, has delivered into our lives and hands, the magnificent gifts that were fashioned in Heaven's throne room to decimate the power of earthly pain.

If not handled correctly, pain can become the defining element in someone's life. Jesus is strongly opposed to allowing the pain of your life to define you; His desire is that you would allow His glorious and matchless gifts to define you in astonishing and prevailing ways. Let's take a lingering and searching look at some of the gifts that have been given to us as we travel this world filled with pain. Among God's abundant and sustaining gifts He generously provides are peace, comfort, and strength.

Peace

"Peace I leave with you, My peace I give to you; not as the world gives do I give to you. Do not let your heart be troubled, nor let it be fearful" (John 14:27).

If the absence of trouble or pain is what you are expecting out of life, there is only one place that holds that infinite promise for you. When we all get to Heaven, we will experience no more sorrow, no more tears, and no more suffering. But while living in the battle zone known as Earth, something more valuable and more eternal has actually been given to us than the mere absence of trouble. We have been given peace in spite of trouble, pain, storms, and war because of the life of and promise of Jesus; we have been given a peace that stands up to pain and says, "I win!"

Jesus himself faced excruciating pain, betrayal by dear friends, physical torture, and loneliness. He was often misunderstood and wrongly accused and yet offers the promise of peace in the very midst of pain to His disciples today. Jesus experienced this extraordinary peace while on Earth's shores and it is His legacy to you. It is His endowment to assuage your very worst moment in life.

Jesus left His peace with us because He wasn't going to need it where He was going. Heaven is already the place of ultimate and eternal peace; Jesus knew that we, His disciples, were the ones who would be grappling with the injustice of Earth-bound living and so He left His peace with us. It is the inheritance of believers to know the peace of Heaven while living in the tragedy of sin, sorrow, and suffering.

A common mistake believers often make is to confuse His peace with the peace the world offers. The world is only able to offer peace in the absence of horrific pain, the nonappearance of gut-wrenching problems, and in the vacuum of severe conflict. God's peace reigns preeminent over any false peace the world could vainly offer because God's peace trumps worry and pain. God's peace destroys anxiety and disappointment. God's peace dominates over trouble and suffering. The peace of God places a restraining order on worry, turmoil, and instability. Whatever this world or the enemy tries to throw into your life, the peace of God is greater still.

Bar the Door

"Do not let your heart be troubled, nor let it be fearful."

These are strong words that echo across the centuries and serve to build a garrison around your life. Jesus and the Holy Spirit are commanding you to take control of your heart, which is the birthplace of your emotions. Refuse to be afraid! Put a restraining order on fear and worry and bar the door to outrageous emotional responses. Even the most mature Christians are guilty of playing with fear and eventually embracing troubling thoughts. The only thing that should be embraced every day of your life is the power found in the Word of God. Unfortunately, we tend to talk about our fears, think about our disillusionments, and rehearse our injustices. We send e-mails overflowing with disappointment, post discouragement and woe on Facebook, and Tweet our troubles. God has supernaturally given the power to control what is happening inside your heart. He has endowed you with the power over all fear. This power is known in as peace, and all that is necessary on your end is to receive this eternal, extraordinary, and all-encompassing gift.

Develop the healthy habits of talking in a peaceful tone of voice and responding to difficult circumstances with a peaceful response. Pray Scripture verses with the word peace in them over your life and over the lives of your family. Choose to be a peaceful person regardless of your past or of the trouble of today.

For the Greeks, peace was defined as "the absence of war," which is a sweet thought but not at all possible. The Hebrew nation defined peace as "the positive blessing growing out of right relationship with God the Father." The greatest Hebrew blessing ever spoken is this one the Lord spoke to Moses and Moses told Aaron to speak over the children of God,

> *"The Lord bless you and keep you; the Lord make*
> *His face shine on you, and be gracious to you; The*
> *Lord lift up His countenance upon you, and give you*
> *peace"* (Numbers 6:24-26).

God, our loving Father, also told His Son, Jesus, to bless you with His peace before He went back to Heaven. God longs for you to embrace the peace of His character and the peace of His presence. God's peace, declares over the life of a believer, "There is nothing to fear. I have been to your future and it is well. I am there."

Triumphant Music

"Rejoice in the Lord always; again I will say, rejoice!"
(Philippians 4:4).

Worship is a prerequisite to peace. If you are having difficulty staying in the oasis of peace and hope, I dare you to worship even when you don't feel like it. I believe worship is the most genuine response when you actually do not feel like worshiping because at that pain-filled moment you are allowing your love for and belief in the Lord to annul the deceit of your emotional response. Peace always follows desperate worship, but will never precede it.

The night the physical presence of the God of the universe arrived on planet Earth in the body of a baby boy, the heavenly messengers sang a triumphant song of joy and peace,

"Glory to God in the highest and on earth peace among men with whom He is pleased" (Luke 2:14).

The victorious symphony of the angels offers us a peek into the birthplace of peace: Peace always follows high worship and an anthem of praise in the night. If you choose to sing rather than panic, the benefit is peace. If you would rather worship than worry, the resulting gift is peace. If you defy your circumstances with your highest praise even in the black of night, you are choosing to accept His wonderful gift of Heaven's entrance into all of your life's circumstances. The gift that is given in exchange for worship is the lavish presence of heavenly peace.

A Beautiful By-product

"The steadfast of mind you will keep in perfect peace because he trusts in You" (Isaiah 26:3).

Peace is not something one should pray for, but in reality peace is a by-product of complete trust in the Lord and in His character. You must first trust Him if you long for His peace. Rather than begging for peace, perhaps a wiser choice would be to worship, to trust, and then anticipate what is given to you in return. Although God's gifts are gloriously free, it has been my experience that they do indeed come with certain strings attached. If you desire peace, you will worship Him in the dark. If you desire peace, you will trust Him when you don't get your way. What I have also noticed about the strings that are attached to God's free gifts is they all lead to intimate relationship with Him. God does not give a gift to one of His children and then walk away, but rather He says, "Let's be friends because I love giving gifts to my friends!"

Walk Gently

"Let your gentle spirit be known to all men. The Lord is near" (Philippians 4:5).

One day when Joy, our fourth child, was about twelve years old, we were walking side by side at the mall. As we walked quickly to meet her older brothers, we weren't talking but just looking in the different windows as we passed. I noticed within just a few seconds that my feet were so much louder than hers. Her steps were measured and landed with such soft grace. My feet were hitting the tile floor hard and rhythmically pounding out a pronounced beat as we walked together.

I commented on the fact that my pace was loud and hers was gentler. My wise twelve-year-old replied, "Mom, that's because we walk differently."

Instantly, I chose to change the way I walked by slowing down a bit and then consciously controlling how hard my feet hit the floor. It took work and focus but I changed the way I walked.

We can all change the way we walk through life with focus and a bit of hard work. You choose whether to pound your way through life making sure everyone hears the rhythm of your being or you can walk with grace, control, and power. You can loudly make your presence known by the choices you make and by rehearsing your pain or you can choose to be gentle and peaceful.

I believe that choosing to be gentle in life is actually one of the strings that are attached to peace. It may take focus and some emotional fortitude, but you actually can choose to be gentle in the words you speak and in the emotions you allow to simmer in the deep places of your heart. You can choose to be gentle or rough in your daily dealings with people. When we consciously choose to be a gentle person, we are choosing to embrace the peace of the Lord. Regardless of your personality type, your ethnic background, or your family heritage, make a determined choice to be a gentle person.

Gentleness should never be confused with weakness because in truth, gentleness implies a reserve of strength that is channeled toward being reasonable and charitable toward everyone. A truly gentle person, who has chosen to reveal this character trait to everyone with whom he or she comes in contact, is communicating that God is in control and there is nothing to be aggressive or pugnacious about.

Gentleness always cultivates strength and beauty in the heart of a believer. If gentleness is a Christian virtue that is difficult for you to embrace, perhaps it would be wise to try to model the life of someone whom you know to be gentle in their dealings with people. Spend time with this compassionate and considerate person of choice and then observe how they respond to others.

"Your adornment must not be merely external— braiding the hair, and wearing gold jewelry, or putting on dresses; but let it be the hidden person of the heart, with the imperishable quality of a gentle and quiet spirit, which is precious in the sight of God"
(1 Peter 3:3-4).

Although Peter was talking to women in his exhortation of gentleness, I believe the principle applies to both genders. The phrase, *precious in the sight of God* is only used one other time in Scripture and in that place it is used to describe the death of the saints. There are some things God values more than others and a gentle spirit is every bit as valuable to God as when one of His dear children comes home to Heaven.

"A gentle answer turns away wrath, but a harsh word stirs up anger" (Proverbs 15:1).

Gentle speaking actually has the power to usher peace into your circumstances in life. Be brave enough to pray this prayer with me today,

"Lord, help me to develop a spirit of gentleness, especially in stormy and difficult situations. Lord, give me the power and the reserve to talk gently and to respond to others in a gentle manner, Amen."

Here is Your Answer!

"Be anxious for nothing, but in everything by prayer and supplication with thanksgiving let your requests be made known to God. And the peace of God, which surpasses all comprehension, will guard your hearts and your minds in Christ Jesus" (Philippians 4:6-7).

If you never seem to have emotional or spiritual peace these two verses hold a miraculous answer for you. These verses, written nearly 2,000 years ago, have what you have been waiting for: specific instructions on how to achieve and maintain the peace of God! It is a two-step formula, sent from the throne room of Heaven, guaranteed to deliver the peace of God into your daily life.

1) Be anxious for nothing.

2) Pray about everything with thanksgiving.

Can it really be this easy? Yes ... it can be this easy ... please don't turn easy into hard. You must deliberately choose not to be anxious, and then reprogram the way you think and process events. You must no longer default to worry and fear, but choose to worship instead. Set your emotional and default settings to "Prayer and Thanksgiving" and then don't ever change them again.

When you resist anxiety with prayer and thanksgiving you will receive the peace that is impossible to understand with human reasoning. This strong peace that is sent into your life from the throne room of God will perpetually stand guard at your heart and at your mind. This magnificent gift of peace will walk back and forth shielding your thought life and your emotions from an onslaught of residual worry and fear. The peace of God will do its job ... but will you do yours?

Will you rejoice over and over and over again? Will you walk gently? Will you stop worrying? Will you pray with heartfelt thanksgiving? The truth of the matter is this:

- Peace is only one worship song away.

- Peace is only one soft response away.

- Peace is only one choice of refusing to worry away.

- Peace is only one thankful prayer away.

Those are the ways we access Heaven's peace while trapped in the war zone of planet Earth. As you determine to put those disciplines of delight into practice in your life, a miracle will happen in your mind and in your heart. The peace will rush in and the worry and anxiety will flee. Don't ever confuse having your own way with the peace of God. Don't ever confuse financial provision with the peace that only God delivers into your life. Don't ever confuse fractious people suddenly becoming friendly as a substitute for Heaven's peace on Earth. All of those things are wonderful and even desirable, but always know God's peace is a blessing and a gift that far surpasses what we see in the natural. God's peace is always delivered with God's power; God's peace is delivered in spite of your circumstances and not because of your circumstances.

Comforted ... not Comfortable

It is a deep and valid human longing to feel comforted by people and to simply know somebody cares when we are traversing days of inestimable pain. Sometimes it is enough just to know that someone with skin on sees what we are going through and then kindly says, "It's going to be OK."

"Blessed be the God and Father of our Lord Jesus Christ, the Father of mercies and God of all comfort, who comforts us in all our affliction so that we will be able to comfort those who are in any affliction with the comfort with which we ourselves are comforted by God" (2 Corinthians 1:3-4).

Many of us grew up with a warped view of God and mistakenly were taught that He was stern, judgmental, and wielded a big stick that would bop us over our heads when we got out of line. We falsely believed God was uninterested in our pain or our daily lives. The words of Paul, inspired by the Holy Spirit, blast that highly false opinion of the character of God into smithereens. Our God ... the God we worship ... the Father who lovingly sent Jesus to give us life ... is actually the Father of mercy and of all comfort. He knows of no other way to be than to be comforting and soothing. It is in His intrinsic nature to reach out to His children with encouragement and love.

Any encouragement you need is from the throne room of God's heart; when you are experiencing traumatic emotional or circumstantial pain, do not make the mistake of attempting to comfort yourself through eating, spending, sleeping, withdrawing, or other temporary panaceas. The God who loves you with every beat of your heart is the Author and Source of all comfort. Nothing and no one else has the power to make any long-term or significant difference in your life. One of the most powerful truths of the abundant life Jesus came to give us is that we serve a God who is concerned ... He simply cares about you.

God not only cares deeply about the things which cause us pain, but He then takes the ugly pain that has penetrated our souls and uses that same wretched pain to turn us into something more beautiful than we were before the pain. He engineers the discomfort into a springboard for our destiny and we are then able to comfort others. Nothing is wasted in the economy of the Kingdom of God as He takes that which was meant to diminish our lives and turns it into profit. God uses broken, pain-riddled lives to bring His healing and miraculous touch to a broken and pain-riddled world.

> Who can best comfort a mother who has lost a child?
> Another mother who has lost a child.

> Who can best give hope to a woman dealing with infertility?
> Another woman who has walked the road of infertility.

> Who can best encourage someone who has lost their beloved spouse?
> Another person who has lost their treasured mate.

> Who can best alleviate the pain of someone who has lost their job?
> Another person who knows the pain of unemployment and rejection.

The abundant life and exquisite joy that is found in the value of being used to comfort another human being is irrefutable.

I am a woman who walked the road of infertility for many, many years. I sent five babies to Heaven who had grown to between twelve and twenty weeks inside of me. After losing five precious babies, I then was unable to conceive and spent years taking high doses of fertility drugs. One of my greatest joys, twenty years after walking the devastating road of barrenness, is the extreme honor of comforting and encouraging women who face the agony of infertility. It miraculously converts the pain I suffered into a meaningful and worthwhile season in my life. Now, because of the opportunity God has given to me to comfort women with the comfort with which He comforted me, I can say I am grateful for those dark days of infertility, pain, and depression. I would go through it all again in order to bring hope and encouragement to those who are treading the waters of infertility.

You will never be able to comfort others unless you first allow the God of all comfort to assuage your weary soul. If you long to be used by God in the long-term of your life, then you will choose to snuggle up to His presence during your worst moments of despair. So many Christians, unfortunately, build a high wall between God and themselves when faced with circumstances beyond their control. Rather than hunker down into the truth of His character and the comfort of intimacy, they embrace anger and hardhearted bitterness.

> I can't go to church ... it's just too hard to answer everyone's questions.
>
> I refuse to call friends for prayer ... they will never understand my pain.
>
> I can't read my Bible ... it doesn't make sense ... it doesn't mean anything.
>
> I am too weary to worship.

If that is your response to the disastrous circumstances of life, then you will stay trapped by the pain much longer than is healthy or holy. You will be held hostage by emotional sewage and the chains of bitterness until at last you run into the arms of the God whose only desire is to comfort you.

We all desire comfort from the people in our lives with whom we feel safe and who love us unconditionally. We are desperate for our spouse, our parents, our children, and our dearest friends to comfort and shelter us in the dark and stormy days of life. When they don't respond in a comforting and compassionate way, we become indignant and angry. However, God will only allow people to do a certain amount for us, and no more. He does not grant people the ability to do for us what only He should be doing. He is the God of all comfort; therefore all comfort we should receive and actually require is birthed in friendship with Him. God is an expert at knowing exactly what we need in every monumental situation in life and He does not want us to replace His comfort with the comfort of people. There are places in our lives that only God is able to fill and into those empty spots He lavishly pours in His perfect comfort.

One of the vital ways God is able to comfort one of His children is when they spend time in the love letter He has written from His heart to your pain.

"My soul weeps because of grief, strengthen me according to Your Word" (Psalm 119:28).

His Word delivers a message of hope and comfort to you at your most painful moment in life's journey. Your flesh may scream at the thought of spending time in God's Word, but it is actually the strongest and healthiest choice you can make at the stormiest moment.

When we allow Him to comfort us in our pain, then we are allowed to comfort others with His healing touch because we have been touched by Him.

It's Time for you to Wait

Do you not know? Have you not heard? The everlasting God, the Lord, the Creator of the ends of the earth does not become weary or tired. His understanding is inscrutable. He gives strength to the weary, and to him who lacks might He increases power. Though youths grow weary and tired and vigorous young men stumble badly, yet those who wait for the Lord will gain new strength; they will mount up with wings like eagles, they will run and not get tired, they will walk and not become weary. (Isaiah 40:28-31)

The strength God gives to those who wait is unlimited and comes in as many ways as there are facets to the eternal character of God. God is lavish in giving emotional strength, physical strength, and spiritual strength. There is no end to His creativity as He gives His fortitude and energy to His children. These matchless verses spoken by the prophet Isaiah nearly 3,000 years ago deliver strength to weary people and power to those who lack might in the twenty-first century.

You are completely mistaken if you believe that strength, vigor, and power are attributes of only the young. If you believe the Bible, then you must also believe that when a person chooses to wait upon the Lord, He will assuredly deliver a new, resilient strength into their personal life. When you pause to access the strength of God and Heaven, you are going to have the capacity to run beyond your human endurance and will not even be out of emotional breath. Your legs will not be weakened nor will your heart be racing with the challenge of it all. You are going to have the vigor to go the distance and then go some more. However, this incredible surge of Heaven's power and strength into your human frailty will only be possible when you choose to wait upon the Lord.

You must eagerly expect and joyously anticipate the promise that God will indeed reward you with His vitality as you read your Bible, as you enter into worship every day, and as you participate in a vibrant and daily prayer life. Those are the disciplines of fortitude that will enable you to not only receive strength from the Lord, but also to apply to your daily walk the strength that you receive. In addition to those helpful and hopeful daily disciplines of power, there might also be times and seasons when you beg directly for God's power.

"God, I need you! This is too difficult for me to do in my own strength. Would you give me your power? Would you give me a word from the Bible I can apply to this situation? I am waiting, Lord, for all that you have for me. In Jesus' name I pray, Amen."

In the Book of Acts, it was when the disciples prayed and waited that they were given the power of Heaven's entry into all of their life's circumstances.

"Gathering them together, He commanded them not to leave Jerusalem, but to wait for what the Father had promised, 'Which,' He said, 'you heard of from Me; for John baptized with water, but you will be baptized with the Holy Spirit not many days from now'" (Acts 1:4-5).

"These all with one mind were continually devoting themselves to prayer, along with the women, and Mary the mother of Jesus, and with His brothers" (Acts 1:14).

The principle of waiting for the power seems not only to be a principle in the in the Old Testament but the theme continues on into the New Testament as found in the potent Book of Acts. The word *waiting* means:

⋮ " ... to expect, look eagerly for, to hope for, lie in
⋮ wait for ..."

When you wait well in the presence of God and are devoted to prayer, you can assuredly anticipate some opportunities that will require the strength of God. Do not use your golden years as an excuse to lie down, give up, or retire because your age has absolutely nothing to do with the energy and vitality that is headed your way from Heaven's resources. God is not done with you yet! Get in the starting gate and in the take-off stance regardless of the date on your birth certificate. Do not sit around waiting to die, but peacefully and hopefully wait for God's strength to overtake your weary bones. Wait on God to give you the strength to literally change the world whether you are fifteen years old ... fifty years old ... or eighty years old.

The word *wait* actually means more than the definition that has been cited; in addition, it also means:

⋮ " ... to bind together, to hold fast to something ..."

If it is strength that you desire, you must bind your life so intimately with God that His strength literally and thoroughly becomes your strength. This term "wait" was used in the ancient Hebrew culture as a gathering of waters. When water is gathered from two separate streams, it is impossible to ascertain which stream the water has come from. When water is poured from two different pitchers into a third pitcher, it is impossible to discern which molecule of water came from a certain pitcher. So it is with the strength of the Lord; when you gather yourself to the Lord and intimately bind yourself to Him, His strength will become your own strength. You won't be able to discern when your strength ends and when His begins!

One of the most miraculous and amazing aspects concerning

the strength of God is that He does not give human strength to His children. He gives of His own divine source of strength. During the difficult days of life, if all you needed were mere human strength, then a self-help guru, a psychology course, or a trip to Hawaii would deliver what you required. However, what you need is a strength beyond human strength; you need more of Him! You desperately need God's strength to be gathered inside of you, and you will receive it while you wait and pray.

Waiting is the string that is attached to strength.

Him, not Me

" ... strengthened with all power according to His glorious might ..." (Colossians 1:11).

All the strength you will ever need to deal with the pain of living this side of Heaven is given according to His glorious might. God has a power source in Heaven that supplies a lavish source of strength and vigor to those who wait for it. When God connects His power outlet with one of His children who has chosen to wait well, He then doles out His strength in profuse and glorious amounts. There is no end to the power God gives to those who expectantly hope for all that He is. God would not know how to give in tiny amounts if we asked Him to ... He only knows of one way to give and that way is according to His glorious might! When one who waits is desperate for strength, God gives all He has and all He is.

He gives strength to love an unlovable spouse.

He gives strength to walk through sickness with joy.

He gives strength to face the holidays with not enough money.

He gives strength to single parents to respond as both mom and dad.

He gives strength to young parents who are weary and stressed out.

He gives strength to singles who are yearning to be loved.

He gives strength to widows and widowers to look ahead and not behind.

He gives strength to couples who are dealing with infertility.

He gives strength!

Peace, Comfort, and Strength

He is the God who gives the peace that passes understanding to those who are in immeasurable pain. He is the Loving Father who gathers traumatized humanity into His arms and sweetly comforts them so they are able to comfort the world in which they live. He is the powerful God of eternity who lavishly supplies strength to those who can't go another mile. Peace, comfort, and strength are your inheritance from the Father as you walk through life in the war zone. These priceless gifts will make your life so much richer, so much more meaningful, and so much more abundant in spite of the pain of your circumstances.

The Rest of Paula's Story

After Paula recounted to me the horror of receiving the phone call that her twenty-three-year-old son had drowned while boating with friends, I gently put my hand on Paula's arm and said, "Oh,

Paula! I am so sorry ... I didn't know ... no one told me."

Although she had tears in her eyes, they didn't run down her cheeks because the sparkle of joy held the tears within her eyes. These were the words of a mother processing the grief of losing her only son,

"Carol, I know my son is with Jesus. Although I would never have chosen this reality, I have peace because of the promises of God. I struggle with happiness, but I am filled with joy because I know I will see my son again. God has been faithful to comfort my broken heart and to give me the peace that passes understanding."

Paula, while working full time in the world of finance, recently earned a master's degree in family counseling. She has felt the tug on her heart to help other families who are experiencing the pain she and her family walked through due to her beloved son's death. Paula knows, because she has experienced the comfort of God, it is now her call and destiny to comfort others with that same comfort. Paula is determined not to waste her pain, but to honor God and her son with the abundance of living a life brimming over with comfort, strength, and peace.

Prayer for Life

"Dear Jesus, I love You so much and I thank You for the gifts of peace, comfort, and strength. Thank You for generously giving all that You have and all that You are to me. In Your powerful name I pray, Amen."

Declaration for Life

"I declare that I will trust the Lord and receive His peace. I declare that I will always worship, learn to walk gently, and pray with thanksgiving so I will receive the gift of God's peace. I declare that I will not push God away while I am in pain, but I will allow Him to comfort me so I can be a comfort to others. I declare that I will wait upon the Lord and gain new strength."

Scripture for Life

"Blessed be the God and Father of our Lord Jesus Christ, the Father of mercies and God of all comfort, who comforts us in all our affliction so that we will be able to comfort those who are in any affliction with the comfort with which we ourselves are comforted by God" (2 Corinthians 1:3-4).

Words of Life

"God cannot give us happiness and peace apart from himself because it is not there; it does not exist."
— C. S. Lewis

CHAPTER EIGHT

Abundant, Lavish, and More!

"LORD, I give up all my own plans and purposes, all my own desires and hopes, and accept your will for my life. I give my life, my all, and myself utterly to you to be yours forever. Fill me and seal me with your Holy Spirit. Use me as you will, work out your whole will in my life at any cost now and forever."

This was the prayer Betty Scott, as an earnest teen-ager, prayed during her first year of college. It was shortly after this she met a young man, John Stam, while attending Moody Bible Institute in Chicago. They were married in 1933, when John was twenty-six and Betty was twenty-seven, and both felt the call to serve as missionaries in China. In the fall of 1934, their daughter, Helen Priscilla, was born and the next month they moved to the remote mountain village in China where they had been called. The village of Tsingteh was only accessible by stone paths cut through the mountains.

John and Betty rented a storefront in which they both lived and held services for the people in the village. The Stams were not the first white missionary couple to visit this village, but they were the first to make it their home.

On the morning of December 6, 1934, when baby Helen was only three months old, there was a knock at the front door of the storefront. Betty was bathing the baby and the messenger at the door announced to John that Communist bandits were on their way to the village. The young Stam family immediately made preparations to leave, but it was already too late. Encouraged by the wild cheering of the people in the village, the bandits broke through the front door of the Stam's home. They were told to take off their clothes and leave only in their undergarments.

The first night they were taken to the local prison where the other prisoners graciously made room for the young family. When baby Helen started to cry, one of the other Christian prisoners asked the guards to at least allow someone to leave with the baby. This prisoner was hacked to death in front of Betty and John and their crying infant.

The following morning, December 7, 1934, John's hands were tightly bound behind his back and Betty was allowed to walk beside him carrying their baby girl. They marched twelve miles in the bitter cold and then were thrust into a mud hut in which to spend the night. Their captors unbound John's hands and he was given the opportunity to write a letter. This is the letter he wrote to the mission board while in captivity:

"My wife, baby, and myself are today in the hands of Communist bandits. Whether we will be released or not no one knows. May God be magnified in our bodies, whether by life or by death. Philippians 1:20."

Sometime during that cold, dark night, Betty looked for the last time at the angelic face of her sleeping baby and nursed her for one last moment. Then Betty bundled Helen inside her blanket and hid her under the covers with two five-dollar bills. The bandits came for John and Betty in the early morning hours of December 8, 1934.

They were marched down the streets of Miaosheo to their deaths while curious onlookers lined both sides of the streets. A compassionate Chinese shopkeeper boldly walked out of the crowd and tried to persuade the Communists not to kill the Stams. The aggressive soldiers ordered the man to go back into his shop; however, he quietly refused. The soldiers then plundered the home of the shopkeeper and found a Chinese copy of the Holy Bible as well as a well-worn hymnbook. The shopkeeper was then bound and led with the Stams to death for the crime of being a Christian.

After marching to the center of the village, John was ordered to kneel and in one swoop of the Chinese sword was violently beheaded. Betty and the shopkeeper were killed seconds later.

More Gifts to Trump Your Pain

What is God's will in the midst of pain and suffering? His will is that His dearly loved children would open and utilize the gifts He has given for such a moment as this. Not only does God unsparingly give the gifts of peace, comfort, and strength, but He miraculously and providentially has other gifts up His magnificent sleeve for His children which will lessen the effects of pain. Into your wretched, un-chosen, and relentless days of pain, God spills wisdom, patience, and joy.

Patience is a Gift

Consider it all joy, my brethren, when you encounter various trials, knowing that the testing of your faith produces endurance. And let endurance have its perfect result, so that you may be perfect and complete, lacking in nothing. But if any of you lacks wisdom, let him ask of God, who gives to all generously and without reproach, and it will be given to him. (James 1:2-5)

James, the brother of Jesus Christ and the leader of the church in Jerusalem, wrote this letter to Christian churches who were suffering severe and intense persecution. To the men and women, some of whom would face beheading, some of whom would be fed to angry and ravenous lions, and some of whom would be burned alive at the stake, James wrote, *"Consider it all joy ..."*

As Christians of the western world in the early days of the twenty-first century, we face stresses, unfair treatment, and major disappointment, but always remember what we are going through does not begin to compare with the unimaginable horror the early Church faced. In our limited view of the mistreatment of believers, most of us know no one who was fed to ravenous lions or who has been imprisoned for the profession of his or her faith. Our major challenges as modern day saints are related to relationship issues, economic woes, raising children in a humanistic culture, and perhaps even agonizing loneliness. When dealing with stress or disappointment, know that if the early Church was encouraged by James and the Holy Spirit to embrace an attitude of joy then their advice to you is exactly the same.

James and the Holy Spirit remind Christians of every epoch in history that the reason we can count various trials as a reason for rejoicing is because " ... *the testing of your faith produces endurance.*" The word endurance used in this verse in the Book of James can also be translated as patience. The Greeks believed that patience was the highest of all virtues and if one only possessed this singular virtue, it would enable the possessor to make it victoriously through life. You are able to miraculously survive any pain that comes against you if you choose to embrace the gift of patience and its twin brother, endurance.

The word endurance in the first few verses of the Book of James is sometimes translated as patience. This Greek word means to: "remain in one's spot, to keep a position, to resolve to maintain the territory that has been gained."

This New Testament power word—endurance—is a word picture of the resolve and determination of soldiers who were ordered to maintain their position in the face of fierce combat. You are the modern day soldier who has been ordered by the Holy Spirit to maintain your position in Christ and in the joy of His presence in the face of fierce and unremitting pain. James and the Holy Spirit agree, that if we are to make it through the fiercest battles in life, we must stand our ground and also defend our joy, peace, comfort, and strength even while the battle is raging all around us.

Out-declare the Enemy

No matter how debilitating the battle may become, your orders from your General are simply to be courageous and survive the attack. His words come ricocheting across the centuries today into your life: hold your position, soldier, because you are going to outlive and outlast the enemy. Your enemy will quickly realize that a soldier of Christ is not going to be defeated and so he will back down and back off simply because you refuse to back down and back off. The words of a joyful, enduring soldier always sound like this:

I don't care how much pain you throw at me, enemy! I don't care how fierce the battle is or how intense your onslaught becomes ... I will not budge one inch. I will choose joy!

And with those power words, you have established your position of endurance and patience. If you are able to face all your trials with endurance, you will have tapped into the staying power of God himself. This type of power holds on, holds out, outlasts, and out-declares the enemy. I hope you have experienced the pure joy of out-declaring your enemy. This is one of the most vital and flat-out fun disciplines of abundant life in which you will ever partake. Your enemy is known for his rotten potty-mouth and his addiction to trash talking. But all that ever comes out of his mouth, regardless of how pretentious and intimidating he sounds, are lies. Complete and obnoxious lies.

The soldiers who are commissioned in the army of the Kingdom of God only declare declarations of truth and faith. The enemy, who is also known as the accuser of the brethren, only deals in fiction and fantasy. Part of the exhibit and practice of patience and endurance is having the tenacity to out-declare your enemy. All the declarations that disciples make are found in the eternal, powerful, and miraculous Word of God.

"No weapon formed against me shall prosper and every tongue that accuses me in judgment God will condemn. This is the heritage of the servants of the Lord" (Isaiah 54:17).

"I can do all things through Christ who strengthens me" (Philippians 4:13).

"He heals all my diseases" (Psalm 103:3).

"My God shall supply all my needs according to His riches in glory in Christ Jesus" (Philippians 4:19).

A believer who wants to do more than merely hope but is determined to fight for victory will make sure the Word of God has been hidden in the deep recesses of his or her heart. The Bible must be the first weapon in your arsenal to which you go when the fiery darts of the enemy are flying in warfare. If you have refused to place the Word of God in your arsenal of defense, you may be caught off guard and then be tempted to fight with unstable emotions rather than with the truth of the Word. Many believers have not taken the time to memorize the Bible and so when Satan begins to trash talk with his venomous supply of outrageous lies, these believers mistakenly feel like defeat is imminent. Out-declare the enemy! Be more relentless, shout out the Word of God decibels louder than he mutters his desperate lies, and then outlast the wimpy voice of the father of all falsehood.

Endurance is the absolute refusal to surrender to obstacles or lying voices. You must determine in your heart that you will emphatically turn down every opportunity to give up or give in. Your only genuine choice is to give all to the King of all kings!

The early Church, influenced by ancient cultures, believed patience was the queen of all virtues. They knew if this royal character quality was ruling in their lives it was no longer a question of *if* they would win, but *when* they would win.

Thinking Like God Thinks

*"But if any of you lacks wisdom, let him ask of God,
who gives to all generously and without reproach, and
it will be given to him"* (James 1:5).

There will be many, many times in life when facing a trial that you will find yourself in need of something in addition to endurance or patience. When you find yourself needing something greater than endurance, what you need is God's opinion on the matter, which is defined as wisdom. You need to be able to think like God thinks.

> God ... how would you pay my bills?
>
> God ... how would you love my spouse?
>
> God ... how would you deal with my difficult in-laws?
>
> God ... how would you respond to my rebellious child?
>
> God ... how would you turn my business around?
>
> God ... how would you make this decision?

As human beings, we all lack wisdom. You are not alone; all of humanity has a deficit when it comes to thinking like God thinks and having His supreme opinion on an issue. One can lack many, many things in life that will affect one enormously, but lacking wisdom may be the most devastating deficit of all.

Lacking money will never impact your life in the way that lacking wisdom will most certainly do. Lacking love or even healthy relationships does not have the power to paralyze forward motion in life the way that lacking wisdom will. Lacking a place to live or an expert doctor's opinion are minimal scarcities when compared to lacking the wisdom of the Father. Wisdom has the solution and the eternal principles that will turn around absolutely any situation in life.

There is only one way to solve the frightening lack of wisdom and that is by simply asking God to supply it. The Greek word used in describing this action of asking is the word *aiteo* and it actually means much more than a gentle ask. Aiteo means to be adamant in requesting and yet doing it with respect and with honor. Aiteo implies that the one asking has a full and definite expectation he or she will receive what has firmly and respectfully been requested.

Often, it seems easier to Google an answer, call a friend, read a self-help book, or panic rather than to pray and aiteo. As believers who want to live a full and abundant life, we must go to God first and firmly ask Him for His strategy and His opinion on a matter.

Your biggest problem is not your problem, but it is your lack of wisdom concerning your problem.

The phrase that is hidden in this powerful initiative from the Book of James brings intimacy and friendship even into the request for wisdom. *"Let him ask of God ..."* is an endearing phrase that in the Greek ushers in the possibility of intimacy with the Giver of wisdom. *Para theou* is a verbal embrace that communicates a very close and intimate relationship with God. It signifies a relationship that means walking as close as possible together. You cannot ask God for something and then think you can just walk casually away from relationship with Him. But as you petition the Creator of the Universe for the privilege of thinking like He thinks, you must attach yourself to Him and determine that you will never walk away from Him and that you will submit your will to His will in absolute agreement.

God is not an information book or the 911 into eternity. You can't just plunk your nickel into the slot machine of Heaven and expect to receive your daily advice for the day. God wants a relationship with you and that is the string that is attached to wisdom. God is not a slot machine, but He's your Dad and He wants you on His lap. When you discover you have a deficit in the wisdom category, position yourself side by side with God and listen intently to His opinion on the matter. God gives to all generously and without reproach because He is the God who is constantly in the habit of giving to His children.

> When God gives
> ... He gives generously
> ... He gives bountifully
> ... He gives abundantly
> ... He gives plentifully
> ... He gives open-handedly.

You can come to your Father without embarrassment and ask Him for His opinion because, of course, we need His help. After all, we are humans and He is God! He doesn't blame us for asking for wisdom or belittle our lack of it. He simply gives it generously because of His love for us and because He is good. There is no such thing as a foolish question in the presence of God because if there were, all of our questions would be categorized as foolish.

And may I just say one more thing about joy and endurance and wisdom? Please do not make the mistake of rushing in and out of the presence of God, but determine to stay with Him long enough to become like Him. Hang out with Him and listen for His wise and caring voice so you are strengthened not only for the moment, but also for the entire day. When a child begins to understand the value of simply being with Dad, the child begins to become like Dad. The child takes on the characteristics, the speech patterns, the habits, and the heart of the Father. You want to be like Him ... trust me. You do.

At the Crossroads of Wisdom, Patience, and Joy

According to the Holy Spirit and James, the gifts of wisdom, patience, and joy all meet in a trial. And apparently, you bring the joy and God supplies the wisdom in that place where endurance, or patience, is developed. If you are the one to supply the joy, where in the world do you get joy at the very worst moment of your life? Is that even possible? Do not falsely assume in these strategic New Testament verses that James is delusional and the Holy Spirit can be deemed as out of touch and inconsequential. No ... think again. Perhaps in these strategic New Testament verses, James and the Holy Spirit are delivering a genuine possibility into the rottenness of your life. James and the Holy Spirit are in agreement that there is more to a trial than simply the trial itself. There is wisdom, there is patience, and there is joy.

Joy Defined

In the fifth grade, my beloved teacher, Miss Sullivan, taught her curious class of eleven-year-olds, that in defining a certain word, one should never use the word itself in the definition. The rule Miss Sullivan taught all of her eager learners is an accepted grammatical rule that all savvy writers and wordsmiths follow religiously. However, it is nearly impossible to define the word joy without using the word itself in the definition.

The Hebrew definition of the word *simchah*, which is translated as joy is this: "joy, mirth, gladness; the joy of God." The Greek definition of the word *chara*, which is translated as joy is this: "joy, gladness; the cause of occasion of one's joy." Due to my frustration at being a wordsmith and knowing that substance is lacking by using the word in its own definition, I decided to dig a little deeper and get to the root of the word joy.

"Joy wrought by the Holy Spirit" was a definition that resonated a bit stronger in my frustrated soul because at least it gave some credit to the Holy Spirit.

And then, at last, I came upon this definition from an old Hebrew dictionary I found among my father's archaic library: "the blessedness that the Lord enjoys." Although this definition uses a derivative of joy in the word enjoys, I found myself completely agreeing with this ancient meaning found among stacks of dusty, dog-eared books.

Joy is the atmosphere of Heaven. It is the air God the Father himself breathes in every day of eternity. And because joy is Heaven's delivered gift to me while I walk on planet Earth, it is my delight and strength to experience the blessedness that God on His throne enjoys. Wow ... put that in your heart and marinate in it!

Joy is God's gift to us as we snuggle into His presence and hunker down into all that He is and all that He gives.

One Choice Away

"You make known to me the path of life; in Your presence is fullness of joy; in Your right hand there are pleasures forever" (Psalm 16:11).

The joy is found wherever He is.

He is in every sunrise and sunset.

His presence is visible in the first flowers of spring and in the glorious leaves of fall.

His voice is heard in the symphony of worship and in the giggle of a baby.

His presence resounds in the roar of the ocean waves and in the majesty of snow-capped mountains.

He is found gently caressing His own in the trauma of emergency rooms and in the aftermath of violent storms.

He ministers to His precious children even while they sleep at night.

He is found comforting widows and brokenhearted parents.

He is on the battlefield carrying a son or a daughter home as the bullets fly and the bombs explode.

He is there in the humdrum of daily life when the dishes are piled high, the laundry is mountainous, and the bills never end. He is there.

He is there in unending days of loneliness and piles of tissues by your bed.

He is with you ... and with Him ... He brings the gift of Heaven's joy!

This verse from Psalms is a stirring reminder when I am being overtaken by the deceit of my emotions that what I really need is more of Him. In order to cultivate the joy of Heaven's grandeur in my puny, ordinary life I need more of His presence and time spent at His beautiful and nail-scarred feet. When my joy beings to fade and is often replaced by loneliness or depression, I am gently reminded by the Holy Spirit that if I am lacking joy ... guess who moved?

All the joy you will ever need this side of Heaven is found in hanging out with Him. It is found when I relentlessly choose more of Him and less of me; it is found when I understand the value of intimacy with the Lover of my soul. If you need joy to be more practical than poetic, perhaps these suggestions will propel you toward the possibility of joy:

- Choose a Scripture that has the word joy in it and memorize it.

- Say it again and again and again.

- Sing a favorite song from when you were a child in Sunday school.

- Sing it again and again and again.

- Whisper a prayer for someone other than yourself.

- Go to church every week and smile at somebody.

- Read your Bible at least three days a week ... then four days a week ... then five days a week ... until you have made it part of the substance of your life.

- Sing at the top of your lungs while you are driving.

- Buy a new devotional and read it every day.

- Invite some people into your home to pray.

Joy is a heartfelt and strenuous discipline that only the desperate are brave enough to choose. I must choose His presence in spite of the world that roars around me. Joy is part of the obedience I make in submission to a God who is always giving to me, always loving me, and always being good to me. For those who lack joy, perhaps part of the dilemma comes from looking for joy in all the wrong places. We mistakenly believe relationships will deliver joy, or that it is possible to purchase joy at the mall along with Gucci, Godiva, and the Gap. We think we will find joy at Disney World or at Harvard. Those pursuits, and many others, will leave you empty and lifeless, but joy will fill you to overflowing and will give you the undeserved, miraculous gift of abundant life. Joy is a choice a believer makes every time His presence is chosen over pain and emotional outrage.

A Baby Named Joy

*"And behold, I bring you good news of great joy
which shall be to all people; for unto you is born this
day in the city of David, a Savior, who is Christ the
Lord"* (Luke 2:10-11).

The eternal reason the angels could announce joy had come to Earth was because joy had come in the person of a Baby named Jesus. This joy, which was delivered that dark, cold night in Bethlehem's manger 2,000 years ago, is so pervasive that every year all of humanity stops to celebrate this birth that changed everything for every person in all of history. Although many people do not even know what they are celebrating, the celebration continues across the ages and across the continents. The world is celebrating the Baby King who was delivered with hope, peace, and joy in abundance. Heaven opened its portals that night and joy splashed into our lives forever. He came into our inky darkness and the joy of Heaven dripped into our world.

The Magnet

*Create in me a clean heart, O God, and
renew a steadfast spirit within me. Do not cast me
away from Your presence and do not take Your
Holy Spirit from me. Restore to me the joy of
Your salvation and sustain me with a willing spirit.
Then I will teach transgressors Your ways, and sinners
will be converted to You.* (Psalm 51:10-13)

I nearly weep every time I read these verses from the Book of Psalms because it once again reminds me of the importance of staying in His presence so I am able to experience His absolute joy. But it is the final line from this particular group of verses that takes me to my knees time after time.

"Then ... I will teach transgressors Your ways, and sinners will be converted to You."

Joy is guaranteed to give you a testimony and to increase your ministry. If you long for your life to make an impact and to change people's lives what must happen first is *you* must be restored to the joy of His salvation. You cannot afford to be an out of sorts, disgruntled, whining, and disappointed believer because there is a world going to hell while you stay sad, miserable, and worn-out. Your joy is the magnet that will draw others to you because they will want what you now have.

I often fly the friendly skies and every time I fly, some size two, perfectly coiffed, woman whose nails never chip and makeup never runs recites these words into the airplane's microphone,

"In the event that our cabin pressure should change, an oxygen mask will be released from the overhead compartment. Please place the oxygen mask on yourself first before helping small children or others who may need assistance."

What is true in the air while ensconced in a flying, metal bird rings true on Earth as you navigate the waters of joy and ministry. You can't help anyone if you are passed out from lack of joy. If you long to help others and make a lasting difference in their lives, then the first habit you will embrace every morning when your feet hit the floor is you will choose the joy of His presence.

Sowing Tears and Reaping Joy

"Those who sow in tears shall reap with joyful shouting" (Psalm 126:5).

If your life has been nothing but pain and sorrow and tears, let me assure you that your life holds more potential for true joy than someone who has lived with a white picket fence guarding the tulips of their life. The Bible says all of your tears are going to miraculously reap a harvest of joy and rejoicing. God takes the tears of disappointment and sadness, fertilizes them with His presence, and out of that place of deep pain will erupt an abundant harvest of joy. You are never immune to this miracle or left out of this promise. Only God can take your worst defeat, your greatest pain, and your moment of raw sorrow and turn it into His miraculous and irreplaceable joy. Only God.

He Died for Your Joy

"Surely our griefs He Himself bore, and our sorrows He carried ... " (Isaiah 53:4).

Not only did Jesus take your sins to the Cross but He also took all your sorrows, as well as everything that has ever made you sad to the Cross. If all Jesus died for was your sins ... it would have been enough ... it would have been more than enough ... but Jesus did eternally more than that. He also took everything that has ever caused you emotional sorrow and everything that will ever cause you emotional sorrow and He died for it on the Cross of Calvary.

Jesus took our sins to the Cross in order that we would experience the freedom of forgiveness and the promise of eternal life. He took our sins to the Cross so sin would no longer have any power over our lives. Jesus took our sorrows and griefs to the Cross in order to replace those painful moments with His joy. The desire of Heaven was that sorrow and grief would no longer hold any power over the lives of God's children, and so Jesus took them to the Cross and delivered the joy of Heaven to planet Earth. It was the greatest exchange in all of recorded history! He took my emotional pain and gave to me Heaven's joy. I don't deserve it ... I didn't earn it ... I don't understand it ... but nothing can change it. His death gave me Heaven's joy! What a completely unpredictable, too-good-to-be-true reality of life on Earth.

Don't Let Go!

"Do not be grieved [or depressed] *for the joy of the Lord is your strength"* (Nehemiah 8:10).

You have an enemy who would love nothing more than for you to live in a constant state of debilitating, relentless depression and discouragement. This enemy is unable to change the fact that you are Heaven-bound and have been guaranteed eternal life. He can do absolutely nothing about your entrance into Heaven's gates. Since he can't touch eternal life, what he attempts to do is to ruin abundant life. Don't let him do it.

You have a God who wants to inject you with His joy because it is God's joy that will give you strength. The devil does not want you strong. This diabolical laughing stock of a shadow wants you to be the weakest version of yourself possible and so he goes about it in one singular way: the devil attempts to steal your joy.

The devil is not after your marriage, your health, your finances, your children, or your relationships. What He is after is your joy and the way that he tries to access your joy is through your marriage, your health, your finances, your children, and your relationships. Do not let the devil have your joy that Jesus died for! Stand toe to toe ... nose to nose ... with the accuser of the brethren and have a stare down. Hang onto your joy and declare in his face,

"Devil, you weak, whining, immature caricature of all that is not holy, you will never ... not ever ... not in a million Sundays ... or in a thousand eternities have my joy. One of us is going down and it ain't gonna be me!"

If you release any of your joy to the enemy it will turn you into a weak, whining, and ineffective Christian because the joy of the Lord is your strength. Your joy is the most valuable commodity you have been given and it is able to give you strength during your days of pain and trauma. If there is anything the devil hates more than a Christian ... it is a joyful Christian. He also despises a peaceful Christian, a patient Christian, a comforted Christian, a strong Christian, and a wise Christian.

The devil will do absolutely anything he can to cut those strings that are attached to God's gifts to you. The enemy does not want you in relationship with Jesus while you are waiting for Heaven. Although it is impossible for him to take Heaven away from you, he will do his devil-best to steal abundant life right out from under your nose. Hang onto peace, patience, comfort, strength, wisdom, and joy. Don't ever let them go because attached to each gift is that string of friendship with God while you wait on planet Earth.

Afraid?

A courageous Christian, Mr. Lo, had followed the bandits who had beheaded John and Betty Stam and the village shopkeeper. When Mr. Lo came upon the gruesome scene, he obtained help from the underground Christian community and placed all three bodies in coffins. Mr. Lo then went to look for the three-month-old baby girl who was still missing. He retraced the steps of the entourage to the mud hut and although over twenty-four hours had passed since Betty and John Stam had left their baby girl, she was smiling and happy under the pile of blankets where her mother had hidden this precious little life. Mr. Lo transported baby Helen to her maternal grandparents who were also missionaries in China.

The coffins of the three martyrs stayed on the hillside of the remote village for forty days until the government released them for burial. Mr. Lo had lovingly sewn their heads back on their earthly bodies and when the caskets were opened nearly a month and a half after their deaths, John and Betty were still clothed in only their underwear, but now were wrapped in white linen and on both of their faces were smiles of expectancy. On December 8, 1943, perhaps John and Betty Stam looked beyond the hate and anger of their assassins and looked into His lovely face where they were greeted by the joy of His presence.

John Stam had written the following poem to his father, Peter, who had been concerned about their safety in the Chinese village. John's wisdom and perseverance are historically recorded in these poignant yet powerful lines:

> **Afraid?** Of what? To feel the spirit's glad release?
>   To pass from pain to perfect peace, the strife and strain of life to cease?
> **Afraid** - of that?
>
> **Afraid?** Of what? Afraid to see the Savior's face,
>   To hear His welcome, and to trace the glory gleam from wounds of grace?
> **Afraid** - of that?
>
> **Afraid?** Of what? A flash - a crash - a pierced heart;
>   Darkness - Light - O Heaven's art? A wound of His a counterpart!
> **Afraid?** Of that?
>
> **Afraid?** Of what? To do by death what life could not -
>   Baptize with blood a stony plot, Till souls shall blossom from the spot?
> **Afraid?** Of that?

Prayer for Life

"Dear Jesus, I love you so much and I thank You for the gifts of patience, wisdom, and joy as I experience the uncertainty of circumstances and sometimes the reality of pain on Earth. I need You more than I need an easy life, a massive fortune, or any creature comforts this world has to offer. I pray, Lord, that You would use me at this moment in history just like You used John and Betty Stam. In Your unchanging name I pray, Amen."

Declaration for Life

"I declare that God has given me wisdom because I have asked for it. I declare that I will stand firm and with resolve regardless of my circumstances in life. I declare that I will choose the joy of His presence every day that I am on planet Earth. I declare that His joy makes me strong!"

Scripture for Life

Consider it all joy, my brethren, when you encounter various trials, knowing that the testing of your faith produces endurance. And let endurance have its perfect result, so that you may be perfect and complete, lacking in nothing. But if any of you lacks wisdom, let him ask of God, who gives to all generously and without reproach, and it will be given to him (James 1:2-5).

Words of Life

"Joy is the infallible sign of the presence of God." — de Chardin

CHAPTER 9

Choose Life ...
Choose Well!

SUSANNAH'S father was a pastor and she was the youngest of his brood of twenty-five children. When Susannah was only thirteen years old, she left her father's church because she disagreed with his theology, so astute was her study and her principles. At the age of nineteen, she married a man, Samuel, who was seven years older than she and together they had nineteen children. Nine of her children died as infants. But the tragic heartbreak of Susannah's life happened when one of her healthy babies was accidentally smothered by a young maid.

Susannah's husband, like her father, was a pastor, but spent a large portion of his adult life in debtor's prison for mishandling the family finances. Their house burned down twice and during the second fire, her son, John, was nearly killed. This gifted, opinionated, godly mother home schooled all of her children for six hours a day. She taught them Greek, Latin, classical literature, math, and science.

Samuel left Susannah for nearly a year because of a disagreement in their marriage. He felt they should pray for the King of England and she refused to pray for such a man. Susannah was unbending in her staunch beliefs and so rather than fight with her, her husband left.

Faced with a life like Susannah's most of us would crawl into a fetal position and stay covered in the blackness of well-deserved depression. However, what one deserves to choose and what one should choose are two different things entirely. What will you choose?

The Power of Choice

We are all given the privilege of choosing what kind of life we will live. It is true we are not always able to choose our exact circumstances, our places of stretching, or even the painful events of life, but we are given the opportunity to choose how we respond to those places of stretching and pain. Every day of your life, you choose.

> You choose whether or not to love Him ...
>
> You choose whether or not to serve Him ...
>
> You choose whether or not to obey Him ...
>
> You choose whether or not to listen to Him ...
>
> You choose whether or not to worship Him ...

Freedom of choice has landed a multitude of believers in every generation in serious conflict with God. If I were God, which I am obviously and definitely not, I am not sure I would have endowed the gift of freedom of choice to humanity. What deeply comforts my questioning soul is the beautiful reason why God was compelled to give all of His dear children the dangerous gift of freedom of choice. God refused to force the object of His love to love Him in return. We must choose to love Him ... or not. Forced love is not genuine love at all, but is a prison of subservience. True love is when the beloved chooses to respond of their own volition and in their own timing to the overtures of the Lover. God's deepest desire is that you would choose to love Him in all of His fullness and glory.

God has not only given us the choice of whether or not to love Him, but He has also given us the astounding choice of whether or not to choose life.

At the Intersection of "My Way" and "God's Way"

The last words a person chooses to speak to the people under his or her care are always layered with significance and heartfelt truth. When a man or a woman knows Heaven is only hours or minutes away, the words that are spoken are carefully constructed and may be among the most vital words of that person's entire life. If you were about to die, what would your final words be to the people whom you loved the most? Perhaps the words that are spoken with one's dying breath are the greatest legacy a man or a woman is able to leave.

Moses, the great statesman, lawgiver, and leader was in just such a position. His days on Earth were coming quickly to an end. In this crucial moment of his life he spoke to the people who would soon be led by Joshua as they went into the land of promise.

> *So it shall be when all of these things have come upon you, the blessing and the curse which I have set before you, and you call them to mind in all nations where the Lord your God has banished you, and you return to the Lord your God and obey Him with all your heart and soul according to all that I command you today, you and your sons, then the Lord your God will restore you from captivity, and have compassion on you, and will gather you again from all the peoples where the Lord your God has scattered you.*
> (Deuteronomy 30:1-3)

God had already warned the people through Moses that when obedience to Him and His Word are refused, ferocious and difficult times are certainly ahead. There are moments in all of our lives when we think we know better than God and blindly hope the rules don't apply to our particular lives. We have our fingers crossed believing falsely that we can get away with sin, disobedience, and questioning God's ways. Every person, however, cannot escape the crossroads of "My Way" and "God's Way." Every person who chooses "God's Way" understands the Father really does know best and the singular priority of life is to honor His Word. God has promised that when you submit your life and your choices to His plan, there will be a blessing on your life that cannot be contained. Your life will not become perfect and trouble-free overnight, but there will be an ease of peace, blessing, and joy that covers even the worst moments of a submitted life.

If you resist the principles found in the Bible and defiantly choose to go down the road marked "My Way," what has actually been chosen is a life of famine and hard living minus the blessing of God. When believers chase down the road of culture and worldly thinking, they are deceived by bright lights and empty promises. The only promise that will be assured in your life is the promise extracted from obedience; the only light that will shine on your pathway is when you choose the pathway of righteousness.

"But the path of the righteous is like the light of dawn, that shines brighter and brighter until the full day" (Proverbs 4:18).

"I'm Home!"

" ... and you return to the Lord your God and obey Him with all your heart and soul according to all that I command you today, you and your sons ..." (Deuteronomy 30:2).

The great news is that when you return to the Lord, regardless of what choices have been made in the past, He welcomes you back with open and loving arms. You simply must say, "Lord ... it's me. I'm home. Forgive me."

Whether you have committed scandalous and glaring sin or have just simply stubbed your toe on sin, the call remains the same. Return to Dad. It is necessary to acknowledge the fact that you have made a poor choice or two ... or three or four ... because returning to Him always involves repenting and asking for His forgiveness.

After you have returned to the Father and after you have repented for past mistakes and choices, then there is still a remaining choice to be made. The third choice is found in whether or not you will obey today. I have found the greatest blessing on my life comes when I choose to obey God wholeheartedly with enthusiasm and even with excitement. True obedience is never accompanied with begrudging behavior or with childish whining. True obedience is accompanied with a choice to love the One who issues the commands.

It's a Pleasure!

"Sacrifice and meal offering You have not desired; my ears You have opened; burnt offering and sin offering You have not required. Then I said 'Behold, I come; in the scroll of the book it is written of me. I delight to do Your will, O my God; Your Law is within my heart'" (Psalm 40:6-8).

God has opened the ears of His children to hear His voice, so do not make it harder than it actually is. You hear His voice while reading the Word of God; you hear His voice in worship, in church, at Bible study, and in prayer. God is a Communicator who loves to speak to His children. When you hear His voice, be delighted to obey.

If God tells you to forgive someone who has been hurtful and unkind to you or to someone whom you love, do it with pleasure. Don't respond to God with excuses or by being defensive. "But God ... do you know how that person treated me? Do you know what they said to me? Do you know how much that hurt me?"

God already knows the person who wronged you does not deserve forgiveness. Do it anyway and do it with pleasure.

When I was a young teenager, there was a swift and serious response in my home when one of us talked back with an attitude to those in authority. If you have not learned this lesson yet in your human relationships, you may never appropriate it to your relationship with God. God knows how that person treated you; He knows what they said to you and about you. As a matter of fact, God knows every sordid detail of every hurtful situation and every tiny innuendo in each inflection in every verbal altercation. God knows and yet still He encourages, "Forgive."

Perhaps God has called you to continue to tithe and to give beyond your tithe even though you are currently strapped financially. When you hear God's voice to give and to tithe, you must obey with delight.

"But, God, this is a tight month and with the holidays just around the corner and with bigger heating bills because it is winter ... I just can't afford to tithe this month. I can't fulfill my commitment to the missionaries. I am sure that you understand."

A mouthful like that is called talking back to God. When God has called a child of His to obey, He truly has taken into consideration all extenuating circumstances in life. You do not need to remind Him why yours is the only life in all of recorded history that does not need to obey. It is vital that you never get into the terrible habit of talking back to God. When you talk back to God and try to reason with Him from a human point of view, it smacks of disrespect and a lack of honor.

Tithing is God's strategy to provide for you in times of economic turmoil and so as you give to God ... do it with delight! It's a pleasure to give to God. Remind yourself not to talk back to God and that it is simply not necessary to tell God your side of the story. Just be delighted to obey ... every day ... all the way. Your life will take a major stride toward abundance when you stop talking back to God and obey with delight.

Once you have made the decision to return to the Lord and then to obey with enthusiastic delight, what happens next?

It's All Coming Back!

" ... then the Lord your God will restore you from captivity, and have compassion on you, and will gather you again from all the peoples where the Lord your God has scattered you" (Deuteronomy 30:3).

It is then your season of restoration begins. Anything you lost because of your sin, because of poor choices, or due to talking back to God will now be restored. Anything you lost, even though it may have been your own fault, will be brought back into your life. God will redeem all the fortunes of your life, which include every aspect of your life that enables you to live a richer life. Anything you have valued or treasured and have lost will be rescued when you come home to God, repent for your sin, and obey with delight. In addition to the reestablishment of your wealth, God, the Father, will comfort you and soothe you. You will find His kind and cherishing touch upon your life. God never gives one of His children the silent treatment nor does He mockingly say, "I told you so! I warned you that if you acted like that your life would fall apart!" God does not continuously scold a truly repentant child of His heart, but He restores your fortunes and then wraps His arms of mercy around you. That sounds like an abundant life to me!

That's Got to Be Painful

If your outcasts are at the ends of the earth, from there the Lord your God will gather you, and from there He will bring you back. The Lord your God will bring you into the land which your fathers possessed, and you shall possess it; and He will prosper you and multiply you more than your fathers. Moreover the

Lord your God will circumcise your heart and the heart of your descendants, to love the Lord your God with all your heart and with all your soul, so that you may live. (Deuteronomy 30:4-6)

What does it mean to have a circumcised heart? That sounds excruciatingly painful to me. Circumcision was part of God's covenant with His people and the first time it is mentioned in the Bible is when God made His covenant with Abram. God had promised Abram that He Himself would multiply Abram and would make him exceedingly fruitful. God promised Abram that kings would come forth from him and God would give him lands and nations. Circumcision was the human evidence that God had made a covenant with His people.

"This is My covenant, which you shall keep, between Me and you and your descendants after you: every male among you shall be circumcised. And you shall be circumcised in the flesh of your foreskin, and it shall be the sign of the covenant between Me and you" (Genesis 17:10-11).

Circumcision is the cutting away of the foreskin on a man's most private and sensitive part. Circumcision cuts away the extra skin and helps to avoid a place where germs can accumulate and potentially cause infection. When you choose to obey God with delight, there will come a time when a cutting away needs to happen in your life as well.

"Moreover the Lord your God will circumcise your heart and the heart of your descendants, to love the Lord your God with all your heart and with all your soul, so that you may live" (Deuteronomy 30:6).

God desires to cut the extra things away from your heart in order to diminish the possibility of germs or infections. The heart is part of the soul, which is the birthplace of emotions, passions, desires, and affections. The soul also encompasses the mind, thinking, and memory. God wants the extra stuff out of your life, which will cause infections, so you are able to love Him with your whole heart. You will never have the capacity or the genuine will to love God with your whole heart until the extraneous is gone from your life. Circumcision hurts when it happens and it may even take some time to heal from that initial hurt. You won't like it when the emotional and spiritual surgery happens and your flesh may cry out in pain and rebellion. And yet, God still says, "Let Me circumcise your heart so that you can love Me fully and completely."

God's desire is to cut away attitudes and habits that may keep Him at arm's distance or that have the potential to cause disease in your life. God only wants the very best for your life and He knows those things that have the capacity to be a hiding place for germs must go in order for you to love Him with your whole heart. It is not going to feel comfortable or be appealing when God says, "It's time for circumcision," but it is also at that moment when the ultimate healing will begin.

The purpose of the circumcision of the heart is "... *to love the Lord your God with all your heart and with all your soul, so that you may live."*

- You need to allow God to circumcise your heart or you will die.
- You need to obey with delight or you will die.
- You need to return to God or you will die.
- You need to quit talking back or you will die.

The Dreaded Root Canal

A few years ago, I had a horrible situation develop in one of my teeth. The aching and the throbbing in this particular tooth were non-stop and it became so painful I couldn't even sleep at night.

The dentist prescribed an antibiotic as well as pain medication for this hot spot in my mouth. However, these prescriptions would only alleviate the pain and infection temporarily. After just a month or two of relief, the pain would come roaring back to the point that my face was swollen and I was unable to eat. My caring dentist then would once again prescribe the pain meds and the antibiotics.

After nearly a year of this relentless cycle, my dentist told me it was time for the dreaded root canal. I resisted nearly to the point of tears, but he firmly told me the only way to stop the pain and infection was to get to the root of the matter.

I must tell you, I would rather go through childbirth than go to the dentist. I despise every single second I spend in that ugly dental chair. In addition to my violent hatred of anything that goes on in the dentist's office, we do not have dental insurance and root canals are very, very expensive. All circumstances were converging into one expensive and painful event that made me cry even to think about it.

My handsome and caring husband, Craig, sat with me in the waiting room and held my cold, clammy hand. When the receptionist called my name she told Craig he could come back in three hours. What? Three hours? Alone in the dentist's chair?

I sat in that chair for what seemed like days, not hours. I felt like the dentist was going all the way into my brain. I had an intense reaction to the anesthesia and spent some of those hours vomiting into a little bowl by the side of the chair. Ah-h-h-h ... the inhumanity of it all! And to top it all off, three hours was only the beginning. It took several way-too-long sessions for the root canal to be announced, "Complete!"

As I left the dentist's office that winter day, glassy-eyed and weary, the receptionist reminded me (after she took my check for over $1,000) to rest for several days and to be very careful about what I ate. I went home, fell into bed, and pulled the covers up over my head. When I woke up the next morning, I felt better and the place where the infection had been no longer throbbed out of control. As the days passed, I realized, "I am better. The infection is gloriously gone! Thank you, Lord, for root canals."

It was worth it to sit in that chair and allow the doctor to do the cutting, removing work that would eventually heal my pain. I knew I never wanted to go through it again, but the end was definitely worth the means. The destination of health and pain-free living was without doubt worth the journey of the root canal.

Circumcision of the heart will be worth it in your life as well. If you can allow God to go to the root of your issues and remove the place of infection, you, too, will finally experience the joy and delight of infection-free living. Allow God to cut away the dead and diseased stuff in your life. When God does open-heart surgery on one of His own children, the end result is abundant life. The healing will provide a freedom that is intrinsically a part of the life of His dreams for you.

Obey Again

*And you shall again obey the Lord, and observe all
His commandments which I command you today.
Then the Lord your God will prosper you abundantly
in all the work of your hand, in the offspring of
your body and in the offspring of your cattle and
in the produce of your ground, for the Lord will
again rejoice over you for good, just as He rejoiced
over your fathers; if you obey the Lord your God
to keep His commandments and His statutes which
are written in this book of the law, if you turn to
the Lord your God with all your heart and soul.
For this commandment which I command you today
is not too difficult for you, nor is it out of reach.*
(Deuteronomy 30:8-11)

This group of verses which resonates from the heart of God down through the centuries and lands with a bulls eye in your life begins with the challenge and command, *"You shall again obey the Lord ... "*

Obedience to God is an issue that should always be at the forefront of all of our lives. After your heart has been circumcised, you are then brought to a new and blessed level of obedience. This new way of obeying brings fresh fulfillment and delight because obedience after circumcision is birthed out of desire, not out of rigid fear.

The definition of the word obey, from the ancient Hebrew, is layered with a series of life-giving events that are guaranteed to take place in the life of one of God's children who understands the power and renewed life of circumcision.

- First, you will *hear* the voice of God and His instructions to you.

- Secondly, you will *understand* what He has said to you.

- Thirdly, you will *hear with interest* His plan for you.

- Fourthly, you will *agree with* the instructions that have been given by God.

- Fifthly, you will *yield to* His amazing and healing plan.

- And finally, you will *obey* from your heart what God "has said.

When a believer has been circumcised and then enters into this delightful way of obedience to God, there is a promised attached as an exciting conclusion.

" ... Then the Lord will prosper you abundantly in all the work of your hand ..." (Deuteronomy 30:9a).

The Lord has an abundant blessing in store for those children of His who are willing to be circumcised and then obey with delight. The Lord has promised to prosper you so abundantly that you will experience the blessing of more than enough. This promise declares *"all the work of your hand"* will be blessed abundantly and you will have leftovers with which to bless others. Everything you set your hand to in obedience, God will cause to prosper in excess. This is a promise most of us long to see fulfilled in our lives, but we refuse to connect the dots between returning to God, repentance, circumcision, and obeying with delight which results in blessing and abundance in life.

"... for the Lord will again rejoice over you for good ...
(Deuteronomy 30:9b).

This is a beautiful picture of the Lord's posture and heart toward you when you have submitted your life to circumcision of the heart and obedience chosen because you want to, not because you have to. When we listen and obey and reveal our love for Him enthusiastically, He prospers our lives and actually sings with joy over us. It is such a humbling thought that dying to self and sin and giving Him my whole heart will actually bring such joy to God, the Creator of the entire Universe! When we choose well, God is thrilled and loves us enough to sing over our lives.

This is a remarkable picture of abundant life:

- You choose to return and obey.
- You allow Him to circumcise your heart - ouch!
- You choose to love and obey some more.
- God sings over your life!

It's Not Too Hard

"... if you obey the Lord your God to keep His commandments and His statutes which are written in this book of the law, if you turn to the Lord your God with all your heart and soul. For this commandment which I command you today is not too difficult for you, nor is it out of reach" (Deuteronomy 30:10-11).

It is not beyond your power, nor is it out of your reach, to return, to obey, to be circumcised, and then to obey and love some more. Some things are definitely too difficult for me. I will never climb Mount Everest or be a daring stunt person or bungee jump into the Grand Canyon. Those things are too difficult for me and are definitely beyond my reach. But God's commandments are not too hard for me nor are they burdensome because God's commandments come with God's grace attached.

There are so many moments in life when it seems too difficult to obey because sin has come calling with a decibel level and a ferocity that cannot be ignored. Satan does not know very many things about abundant life, but one thing he does know—you have been given the power of freedom of choice. The enemy, the deceiver of your soul, attempts to attract your attention in every human and demonic way possible. He proclaims and encourages; he deceives and shouts and whispers; he promotes and exaggerates and pontificates. This scrawny, washed-up bag of bad breath gets louder and more obnoxious every time he observes that you are still trying to make up your mind about whether you will choose your way or God's way.

There is one habit that will shut up old Mr. Falseface in an instant of time: when you determine to read the Bible, you are stuffing a sock in the mouth of the enemy. When you choose to intensely listen for God's voice and spend time in worship and prayer, the devil turns tail and runs. If you genuinely love someone, it shows in big and little ways. Our obedience to the Father and to the Son is the litmus test of our love for them.

"If you love Me, you will keep My commandments"
(John 14:15).

I choose to love Him and then to show it through my actions and through the decisions I make. My flesh may scream in absolute and agonizing pain, but I love Him so I will obey with delight.

- Returning and obeying ... I can do that because I love Him.

- Circumcision of the heart and obeying ... I can do that because I love Him.

Write Them on My Heart

*See, I have set before you today life and prosperity,
and death and adversity; in that I command you
today to love the Lord your God, to walk in His ways
and to keep His commandments and His statutes and
His judgments, that you may live and multiply, and
that the Lord your God may bless you in the land
where you are entering to possess it.*

*But if your heart turns away and you will not obey,
but are drawn away and worship other gods and serve
them, I declare to you today that you shall surely
perish. You will not prolong your days in the land
where you are crossing the Jordan
to enter and possess it.*

*I call heaven and earth to witness against you today,
that I have set before you life and death, the blessing
and the curse. So choose life in order that you may
live, you and your descendants, by loving the Lord
your God, by obeying His voice, and by holding fast
to Him; for this is your life and the length of your
days, that you may live in the land which the Lord
swore to your fathers, to Abraham, Isaac, and Jacob,
to give them.* (Deuteronomy 30:15-20)

God has given us the freedom to choose life and prosperity or death and adversity. Every time you choose your own way rather than God's way, what you are choosing in reality is death and adversity over the promises and the blessings of God. It is not too difficult for you to choose to love the Lord, to walk in His ways, and to keep His commandments. When you make that choice, the blessing is enormous.

From the day each one of my five rambunctious, creative children turned the dreaded age of two, I taught each one "Delayed obedience is disobedience." God desires this same type of immediate and heartfelt obedience just because you love Him and are in friendship with Him.

- If God has told you to ask someone to forgive you ... just do it!

- If God has told you to give more than your tithe ... just do it!

- If God has told you to break off an unhealthy relationship ... just do it!

- If God has told you to bless someone ... just do it!

- If God has asked you to allow Him to circumcise your heart ... just do it!

If you choose not to obey the voice and the commandments of the Lord, you will pay a far greater price than you are able to afford. The price you will pay is death to an abundant life and you will unfortunately be forced to welcome adversity rather than prosperity and blessing. Conversely, when there comes a time in your life when you realize you need multiplication on any level, it is at that moment God will lead you to deeper levels of obedience. Deeper levels of obedience always produce greater multiplication of blessing and abundance in the life of a believer.

As you look at the options and choices that are presented during your stay on planet Earth, the Holy Spirit and Moses are in agreement that you should resolutely choose life by loving God with reckless abandon and absolute obedience. When you open your heart fully to God and respond to His love, you will be the recipient of the greatest life imaginable. It's not that your circumstances are guaranteed to line up to human perfection. However, during the moments when life's circumstances and events are at their worst, God will usher in His grace, His favor, and the promise of the miraculous. If you long to live the very best life possible during your tenure on Earth, then you will choose to obey without delay and also you won't talk back disrespectfully to God. You only have one life to live and this is it. Live well and choose well. Love God well! When you love God with deep commitment and enthusiasm, you are choosing life in its fullest measure.

Susannah

Susannah Wesley was known by all as a woman who held the Word of God in high esteem. Every day, regardless of what was going on in her home or in her life, she would spend two hours of study in the Bible. In addition to the delight of reading the Scriptures, Susannah had a rich and vibrant prayer life that nothing was allowed to interrupt.

Susannah pastored the church held in the family home in her husband's oft absence and the people loved to hear her insight into the Scriptures. When Samuel was in attendance to pastor the church, it would dwindle to nearly no one other than family. However, when Samuel was away and Susannah was given the opportunity to preach a lively sermon, the church would swell to over two hundred in attendance in their home.

Not only did Susannah pastor their church, teach the children, run the farm, and keep food on the table, but she was also a student of theology and scriptural commentaries. She actually wrote commentaries on the Apostles Creed, the Ten Commandments, and the Lord's Prayer while raising her large and boisterous family.

This woman, Susannah Wesley, was an extraordinary combination of wit, compassion, opinion, and deep thinking.

Most women who were forced to live her life of poverty, with an absentee and inattentive husband, a house filled with children, and sending nine babies to heaven, would have curled up into a fetal position and emotionally died. But not Susannah Wesley. Susannah chose to stay engaged with the life she had been given and to live wholeheartedly for the Christ of the gospels.

Two of her sons, John and Charles, brought revival to the newly birthed United States of America. They wrote hymns that are still widely sung today and books that are considered classical Christian theology and literature. John and Charles Wesley are esteemed as two of the most influential Christians of all time.

Susannah refused to be trapped by the quicksand of her devastating circumstances and chose to love and obey God even when her world was falling apart. Susannah held fast to God and to His promises in spite of deep emotional pain and rejection. The legacy of Susannah's life echoes through the centuries as a powerful testament to the blessing and abundance of God when one person chooses to love God unremittingly.

We all have a choice ... what will you choose?

Prayer for Life

"Dear Jesus, I love You so much and today I choose You. Please forgive me for my sins and help me pursue You with love and obedience. I don't want my will but I want Your will in all that I do. Thank You for the abundant life You have given to me. In Jesus' name I pray, Amen."

Declaration for Life

"I declare that I will return and obey God. I declare that I will love Him enthusiastically and that I will obey Him again. I declare that this is not too difficult for me to do. I declare that my life will be a glorious show and tell of the riches and favor of God."

Scripture for Life

"... if you obey the Lord your God to keep His commandments and His statutes which are written in this book of the law, if you turn to the Lord your God with all your heart and soul. For this commandment which I command you today is not too difficult for you, nor is it out of reach" (Deuteronomy 30: 10-11).

Words of Life

"Oh, the fullness, pleasure, sheer excitement of knowing God on Earth!" — *Jim Elliot*

CHAPTER 10

A Life of Miraculous Intervention

NELSON BOYCE started a family business with his father and brother. They sold biscuits, crackers, and bread out of three wagons in New York, Rhode Island, and in parts of southern Canada. One of the most successful products they made was a cookie that consisted of two chocolate wafers with vanilla cream in the center.

Nelson lost his first wife in childbirth and had raised his two sons alone. When his sons were nearly grown, Nelson married a woman twenty years his junior and they began their family in the mid-1920s in western New York. Because of the success of their business, his young wife and daughter enjoyed a life of comfort and luxury. He employed a fulltime maid as well as a nanny to help his young wife make the adjustment to married life. Mary, Nelson's wife, was known for her fashion flair and was always dressed in the latest style.

However, the Boyce family, which was respected for their business acumen and astute economic sense, saw the Depression coming and so rather than lose their business, they sold it while they could still make money from the sale.

Nelson, with his part of the profits of the sale of the biscuit company, bought a general store and a simple family home in a small town in western New York. The Depression hit this small town with devastating effects and the little general store struggled to stay afloat in the worst economic days America had ever experienced.

By the mid 1930s, Nelson had three young children to support as well as his wife. This family who had been accustomed to designer clothes and maids now wore patched clothing and lived like most other families did during these days of economic woe, with never enough to eat. But Nelson made sure that his family knew the joy of faith, giving to others, and togetherness. He was determined that what he was unable to offer in material goods he could more than make up for with his undivided attention and unconditional love.

You are the Masterpiece and the Miracle

God has been dreaming about your life before the creation of the Earth. Before there were cockatoos, orchids, or waterfalls, you were in God's heart. Before Abraham took Isaac up the mountain, before Moses split the Red Sea, and before David hit a bull's eye on the forehead of Goliath, God was intensely planning your life. God arranged all of history for your grand entrance upon this war zone of Earth.

For You formed my inward parts; You wove me in my mother's womb.
I will give thanks to You, for I am fearfully and wonderfully made;
Wonderful are Your works, and my soul knows it very well.
My frame was not hidden from You, when I was made in secret,
And skillfully wrought in the depths of the earth;
Your eyes have seen my unformed substance;
And in Your book were all written the days that were ordained for me,
When as yet there was not one of them.
(Psalm 139:13-16)

You have been fashioned and crafted by God for such a time as this; history would not be complete without the days, the contribution, and the impact of your singular life. You have been made by God, and all of His works are wonderful indeed! God has an extraordinary life chosen for each one of His beloved children who have been made in His image. The life God has created for you is a life overflowing with His presence, His power, and His joy.

The question remains: If God is so good why do I continually deal with lack and storms? Is there a part of abundant life that has been withheld from me for some reason I just don't understand? If God pre-arranged history for my grand entrance, why does everything seem so continuously difficult and perplexing?

God desires for His children to look beyond the storms and the days of lack to discover His fingerprint in those very moments of life. There is the potential for miracles in all of life's challenges. The Bible is not fairy tale, fantasy, nor is it fiction, but it is an accurate historical account of the move of God during recorded times. A major component of the promise of the gift of abundant life is not just the mere possibility of miracles, but the guarantee of them! Jesus did not stop performing miracles just because His location changed from Earth to Heaven.

"Jesus Christ is the same yesterday and today and forever" (Hebrews 13:8).

The Whole Truth and Nothing but the Truth

"Truly, truly I say to you, he who believes in Me, the works that I do, he will do also; and greater works than these he will do; because I go to the Father" (John 14:12).

Jesus told the truth when He declared to His disciples that because He would be returning to Heaven to be with the Father, His disciples would have the guarantee of the greater works. Because you are a disciple of Jesus Christ, and because we know He does not change, but is the same yesterday, today, and forever, you have the promise of doing greater works and seeing greater miracles. Anything Jesus did while on Earth ... you can do better and greater! The miracle of the greater work is not because you are in any way better or greater than Jesus, but it will happen because Jesus said so and He always tells the truth.

Miracles are one of the ways that Jesus deals with lack in our lives. If you are lacking health, relationships, financial provision, direction, peace, or joy, you can expect the God of promise and miracles to interject His answer into your life today.

It's Not About Me

"Now when Jesus heard about John, He withdrew
from there in a boat to a secluded place by Himself;
and when the people heard of this, they followed Him
on foot from the cities" (Matthew 14:13).

Jesus had just received the news that his childhood companion and cousin, John, had been senselessly murdered. Jesus needed a place of seclusion and solitude to process the pain of Earth and to grieve the life of his dear friend. But Jesus could not get away even in a time of tragedy. The crowds were still able to sniff Him out and followed Him to His quiet place.

"When He went ashore, He saw a large crowd, and
felt compassion for them and healed their sick"
(Matthew 14:14).

This verse clearly demonstrates the compassion and heartfelt concern for others Jesus lovingly chose at this moment of pain. He wanted to be alone because He was in mourning, but mercy triumphed over mourning. Jesus knew that even in one of life's darkest hours He was on planet Earth to heal the lives of broken and diseased people.

Perhaps it is how you respond while in a trial that reveals whether you are self-centered or are compelled by the compassion of Jesus Christ. Mercy always leads to loving ministry while solitude is always driven by selfishness. There comes a time during dark days of grief and mourning when we all must lay aside the solitude and reach out to others. God cares about others; this is a message that never changes. Jesus, the Son of God, made the most of every opportunity, even when in His flesh He desired to be alone. If you are desperate for a miracle, you might start by being an unselfish person and by reaching out in compassion and mercy toward others who are watching your life.

> When someone has a need ... meet it.
>
> When someone is in pain ... don't just talk, but listen with your heart.
>
> When someone is sick ... pray for them and take them a meal.

Faith, Facts, and Fiction

"When it was evening, the disciples came to Him and said, 'This place is desolate and the hour is already late; so send the crowds away, that they may go into the villages and buy food for themselves'"
(Matthew 14:15).

The disciples were just so human, weren't they? They definitely were not chosen to be disciples because of their faith or their compassion; these boys had so much to learn!

The disciples started this confrontation with Jesus by telling Him where He was ... as if Jesus had not yet recognized the fact that He was in a desolate place! And then, they informed Him what time it was. They told Jesus, who was there when His Father flung the sun, moon, and stars into place, that the hour was getting late. Time was God's idea and these micro-managers were compelled to point out the obvious.

It was like telling Einstein that 2 + 2 = 4.

It was like showing Beethoven where middle C is on the piano.

It was like instructing Rembrandt how to draw a stick figure.

And then, these brilliant specimens of humanity told God, who was there in the flesh, how to handle a difficult situation. The God who has plans for welfare and not for calamity didn't need the advice of a band of brothers who walked by sight and not by faith.

The disciples were focused on their lack ... what they did not have. The disciples were fact-oriented and Jesus always calls His disciples out of the facts of a situation and into a place of faith in His character and in His power. The disciples were consumed by their circumstances and Jesus was consumed with compassion.

In effect, what these ludicrous and aggressive young men were saying to Jesus was this, "You have preached and ministered way too long. We are going to have a hungry mob on our hands!"

The disciples were walking by the facts of their situation, which was rife with lack; doing this will always cause a disciple of Christ to be frustrated with the Lord and then this misguided disciple will begin to tell Jesus what to do. Believe me ... God does not need your advice.

The disciples chose to walk by sight, but Jesus saw by faith what they were refusing to see: Jesus saw the makings of a miracle. Telling Jesus what to do and apprising Him of situations and circumstances is just not necessary. The disciples focused on what they did not have rather than on who they were with!

Lack + Jesus = Miracle

It did not matter to Jesus that the hour was late and there was no McDonald's on the corner: what mattered was His compassion and His power. If you long for a demonstration of Heaven's power then you must not look at what you have or at what you do not have.

You must look at Who you are with.

Don't look at where you are ... look at Who you are with.

Don't tell God what time it is ... look at Who you are with.

God's Opinion

*"But Jesus said to them, 'They do not need to
go away; you give them something to eat!'"*
(Matthew 14:16).

Jesus rarely agrees with our human answers to difficult situations in life. Do not expect God to agree with your human appraisal of life's events because He simply does not look at life the way most human beings do. Humans see all the frustrations and God only sees all His answers to our frustrations. Jesus, tapping into the wisdom of God in this situation, decided to involve these faithless, fact-filled men in the answer to this dilemma. Jesus could have provided for the situation of lack without them, but He chose to involve them in a miracle. Jesus is still doing that today, nearly 2,000 years after this event took place. Jesus is still inviting faithless, fact-filled men and women to partner with Him in the miraculous. If you are dealing with a situation that is rife with lack and poverty today, begin to give yourself away to others. It is where the miracle begins.

"I will bless you ... and so you shall be a blessing
[to others]" (Genesis 12:2).

"Only" is not in Heaven's Dictionary

*"They said to Him, 'We have here only five loaves
and two fish'"* (Matthew 14:17).

"Only" is not in the vocabulary of Jesus. It never has been and it never will be. Jesus does not know what an *only* is because He is the God of abundance. Only is a word of humanity while *abundant* is the word of Divinity. When Jesus is involved in your life, all things identified as only are about to be touched by the miracle of abundant!

"And He said, 'Bring them here to Me'"
(Matthew 14:18).

Bring all of your onlies to Jesus and just see what happens when He touches an only with His abundance. Only is merely enough to feed one young boy, but when only is touched by Jesus, it becomes enough to feed a ravenous, frustrated, demanding, and tired mob!

Three Keys to a Miracle

"Ordering the people to sit down on the grass, He took the five loaves and the two fish, and looking up toward heaven, He blessed the food, and breaking the loaves He gave them to the disciples, and the disciples gave them to the crowds" (Matthew 14:19).

In this amazing verse are hidden the three keys to a miracle. Watching the life, hearing the words, and imitating the actions of Jesus on this particular day are what it takes to participate in a miracle at a moment of frustration and lack.

1 - Look up!

You will never partner with Jesus in a miracle if you only see what is in your hands. You must set your gaze on Heaven's power and remind yourself that there is a God who does indeed dabble in the affairs of mankind. There is a God who is more than enough in any of your life situations. There is a God!

2 - Bless!

As you partner with Jesus in bringing a touch of Heaven to

Earth, begin to pray and give thanks. Worship with your whole heart knowing God is well-able to match His abundance with your *only* and a miracle will result. Worship is the atmosphere where miracles thrive and is the Petri dish where miracles are conceived.

3 - Start to give!

Generosity is the fertilizer for a miracle that was conceived in the soil of worship. A miracle is not about what you have or do not have at your disposal to selfishly keep and horde, but a miracle is about what you choose to give. When you choose to give what has been placed in your hands, you are revealing the heart and character of God and a miracle is only moments away. Jesus wanted the disciples to be part of the miracle. Jesus wanted to release them from a robotic mindset, mindlessly reciting everything within seeing distance. If all you are doing is reciting your problems you will never experience the miraculous. Partner with God in lavish giving and watch the miracle happen in your own hands. Those greater works that Jesus promised will only be an elusive and hoped for dream unless you choose to give away what is in your hands.

> *"Give and it will be given to you. They will pour into your lap a good measure—pressed down, shaken together, and running over. For by your standard of measure it will be measured to you in return"*
> (Luke 6:38).

Did you know that there are three exciting impossibilities in life?

  You will never be able to out-love God.

  You will never be able to out-dream God.

  You will never be about to out-give God.

I dare you ... try it ... and watch the miracle that will take place in front of your very own eyes in your very own hands.

All!

*"And they all ate and were satisfied. They picked up
what was left over of the broken pieces, twelve full
baskets"* (Matthew 14:20).

Do not make the sad mistake of only reading this spectacular
verse historically. Read this verse personally and enthusiastically.

"And they *all* ate and were *satisfied*. They picked up what
was *left over* of the broken pieces, *twelve full baskets"*!

These fact-chained boys did not merely hand out hors
d'oeuvres to the starving crowd. This was not a meager display
of peanut butter and jelly sandwiches, but a bona fide, miraculous
Thanksgiving feast before their very eyes. There would be leftovers
for days because Jesus was there. There was one basket left over
for each of the disciples. I wonder, if, as Jesus handed a basket
to each one of the fact-filled men, if there was a gleam in His eye
as He said,

"Matthew ... try and count what is left over in
this basket!"

"Luke ... this food will heal you!"

"Thomas ... can you believe it? Leftovers!"

"Peter ... I hope that you will always remember
who I am."

"John ... now you know my love for you."

A Gargantuan Blessing

*"There were about five thousand men who ate,
besides women and children"* (Matthew 14:21).

Theologians and historians believe there may have been as
many as 20,000 people there that day who were fed on five

little rolls of no significant size and two dried-up fish. May I just remind you, if you are only looking at what is in your hand, you will experience continual frustration? However, if you will look to Heaven and worship and then be extravagant in your giving the blessings will be gargantuan! There will be no way to measure the enormous miracle that will happen because there will be leftovers in abundance. The miracle is never found in the size of the loaf, but in the power of the Lord who is with you.

Time on the Mountain

"Immediately He made the disciples get into the boat and go ahead of Him to the other side, while He sent the crowds away. After He had sent the crowds away, He went up on the mountain by Himself to pray; and when it was evening, He was there alone"
(Matthew 14:22-23).

Immediately Jesus compelled the disciples to get into their boat and go across the Sea of Galilee. The crowds had been pressing in on Jesus and the Gospel of John tells us at this moment they wanted to make Him king. Jesus sent the people away because He desired to go to the mountain to pray.

Finally, after a long day of dealing with opinionated disciples and the needs of the multitude of people who were following Him around, He was at last able to go to the mountain to pray. Jesus needed extra time with His Father that day as He processed the death of His cousin, John the Baptist.

Never underestimate the healing power of being with the Father in prayer as you process the things that cause you grief and sadness. If Jesus needed time alone with the Father, we need it in exponential proportions. Jesus ached for these powerful moments of fellowship and intimacy with His Dad and so should we. The problem with us is we try to fill that same ache with the earthly solace of habits. Nothing will comfort you like time spent on your knees in His presence. Send everyone and everything else out of your life and make it a priority to go to the mountain of prayer.

What a Boat!

"But the boat was already a long distance from the land, battered by the waves; for the wind was contrary" (Matthew 14:24).

Oh, how I love this little boat! I wish I could just have one piece of splintered wood from this boat that was rocked to and fro by the contrary winds of nature. Perhaps this was Peter's boat before He heard the Lord's voice calling His name. This little boat had soaked up the tears Jesus cried after He heard of the death of His beloved cousin who had made a way in the wilderness for Him. Jesus had preached many sermons from this little boat so the crowds could hear His voice. Now, this little boat, which represented their former way of making a living to some of the disciples, is about to see a miracle that has been remembered over the course of 2,000 years.

The disciples had been sent away from Jesus in order to travel across the water before the sun had set that day. This boat had probably begun its journey before 6:00 p.m. There are three significant facts to observe as we begin to view the makings of another miracle:

1) The boat was a long distance from land.
2) The boat was being battered by the waves.
3) The boat was in the midst of a contrary wind.

Your life may be experiencing the exact same weather conditions as did this little wooden boat. Perhaps you are not where you think you should be because you believe your life has run off course. You may be wondering if anyone understands how far away from stability and security your life has wandered. You may feel your life has been battered by the storms and waves of life. You may even be experiencing the tremendous strain of a life literally torn apart by relentless circumstances and events. And finally, even now, you know you are in the midst of a driving and contrary wind. Your life may be totally out of control and you know that if something does not stop the storm soon, you will be fighting for your very existence.

"And in the fourth watch of the night He came to them, walking on the sea" (Matthew 14:25).

The fourth watch of the night was between 3:00 and 6:00 a.m. The disciples had been battling the storm for perhaps as long as twelve hours and their options for safety had run out. You may literally be in the same boat as the disciples. You may be exhausted from having fought the effects of the storm, waves, and wind in your life beyond what is humanly possible.

The last time the disciples had encountered a storm of this magnitude, Jesus had been in the boat with them (see Matthew 8:23-27), but this time they are all alone. Perhaps Jesus was hoping these men, who insisted on walking by sight and not by faith, had learned a lesson or two by now. Maybe when Jesus was on the mountain praying to the Father, He was praying for this group of a dozen disciples whom He had chosen. Jesus may have been hoping they would remember the words He spoke the last time they were caught in the middle of the sea by the tumultuous storm,

> *"Peace! Be still!"*
>
> *"Why are you afraid, you men of little faith?"*

A Cake Walk

Jesus came walking across the raging seas toward the storm-tossed and weather beaten boat. This was no short and easy jaunt, but it was almost a three to four mile hike across angry, tempestuous waters. Jesus was probably covered by the spray of the water and the sand as it was driven by the wind. And yet He kept walking with one thought in mind, "I must get to my boys."

> What is impossible to man is a cakewalk to God!

> What causes us to fear is a walk in the park to Him!

> What we are overwhelmed by, He controls!

And yet, as Jesus came walking across the boiling and turbulent water, drenched to the bone, He had not yet calmed the sea. He could have done it from the shoreline; one word from the Man who created this puddle and it would have instantly been still.

"When the disciples saw Him walking on the sea, they were terrified, and said, 'It is a ghost!' And they cried out in fear" (Matthew 14:26).

Sometimes Jesus appears in ways that are impossible to understand from a human perspective. Oftentimes, in the middle of out-of-control emotions, we mistakenly accuse Him of being something He is not. The waves were endangering the lives of the disciples but Jesus used those same waves as a vehicle upon which He would walk into their storm. There are people whom we dread and circumstances we fear and unfortunately our response to these people and circumstances may be flailing and fallible emotions. However, it is through that which we fear the most that the greatest blessing of our lives may come if we will recognize His Lordship.

"But immediately Jesus spoke to them, saying, 'Take courage, it is I; do not be afraid'" (Matthew 11:27).

And still, Jesus has not calmed their storm. Before Jesus deals with the storm of your life He will first confront your fear issues. He wants you to be more aware of His presence than you are of the storm that is throwing you around. When you have been battered and are dealing with the results of a contrary wind, the miracle that happens first is His peace is pronounced over your life as a result of His dear presence.

I Want What You've Got

"Peter said to Him, 'Lord, if it is You, command me to come to You on the water'" (Matthew 14:28).

I love Peter. He is my favorite disciple. I have often prayed, "Lord, when I am in storm, give me the faith of your buddy, Peter."

Peter wanted to do what Jesus was doing. He longed for the miraculous power of Jesus to be demonstrated in his life. Peter was the only one of the twelve disciples who wanted the greater works. He was the only one who asked for it. The other disciples were in the weakened boat wiping their brows and taking one another's blood pressure. Perhaps they were reminding one another, "Breathe in ... breathe out ... breathe in ... breathe out."

But Peter who was the man of adventure and faith recognized this moment as the opportunity of a lifetime. He could be part of the demonstrative miracle of Jesus and boldly proclaimed, "Jesus! I want what you've got."

"And He said, 'Come!' And Peter got out of the boat, and walked on the water and came toward Jesus. But seeing the wind, he became frightened, and beginning to sink, he cried out, 'Lord, save me!'" (Matthew 14:29-30).

When Peter took His eyes off Jesus and became more aware of the storm than he was of His Savior, it was at that instant Peter began to sink. As Peter looked at his circumstances, he saw the force of the wind, and then he became frightened and began to sink. If you are more aware of your circumstances than you are of the presence and power of Jesus, like Peter, you will be overcome with fear and find that you are in way over your head. What holds you up is your faith. What keeps you from drowning is an awareness of Who is with you. The Man who made the seas has more than enough power to calm the seas. Never confuse where the power lies: it lies not in the storm, but in Him.

"Immediately Jesus stretched out His hand and took hold of him, and said to him, 'You of little faith, why did you doubt?'" (Matthew 14:31).

Jesus is always ready to catch us when we falter. He is always ready to save us in spite of the strength of the storm in which we find ourselves. He is always ready to protect us regardless of the size of the waves threatening our lives. Peter never should have taken his eyes off of Jesus, but when he did, at least he quickly corrected himself with the words that hundreds of thousands of others have cried, *"Lord! Save me!"*

"Jesus! Save me!" is an effective prayer to pray when you have taken your eyes off Jesus. Look for His almighty hand and stretch out your hand to meet His capable and caring grasp. Jesus is actually very good at saving disciples who are in over their heads. Maybe it's because He has had to do it so often.

At Last

"When they got into the boat, the wind stopped"
(Matthew 14:32).

Only when Jesus and Peter got back into the boat did the wind finally stop its howling. Jesus wants you to be more aware of His presence than you are of the storm rocking your boat. Wherever the presence of Christ is known and recognized, the wildest storm ceases to rage.

> *"And those who were in the boat worshiped*
> *Him, saying, 'You are certainly God's Son!'"*
> (Matthew 14:33).

Every storm experience in your life should end in worship and in the recognition of exactly who He is. Never leave the storm without spending time in heartfelt worship as you declare for the world to hear who you know Him to be. When the winds stop howling, and they will ... and the waves cease crashing, and they will ... when your boat stops rocking, and it will ... spend time in complete adoration to the One who speaks peace to every storm.

A Desperate Situation

Nelson Boyce, the father of three and a small business owner, was desperately trying to make ends meet while keeping the doors of his country store open. Then there were the fierce days of winter to deal with as well. How would he keep them warm with no money to buy coal?

Nelson would pour over the accounting books of his struggling store in his dark, cold office and ask God to make a way where there seemed to be no way. He kept his Bible open on the desk and often read the Word of God to fight off the fear of poverty, of starvation, and the cold.

Nelson's general store was right on the edge of an Indian reservation and one day when Nelson was in his office looking over the books, a family of Indians walked into the store and asked to see Mr. Boyce. The humble father of the family told Nelson his children were starving to death and wondered if they could buy food on credit.

Not hesitating a minute, Nelson loaded up their ancient truck with groceries and had them sign their name with an "X" because neither the mother or father knew how to read or write. He assured them they could pay him when they had the money.

The next day two more families came from the reservation and by week's end, Nelson had given groceries to nearly a dozen Indian families. The conversation was always the same, "Sign your name with an 'X.' You can pay when you have the money."

Although this made no sense in the natural, the economy of God has never made sense in the kingdoms of this world. Right in the middle of the Depression, the Alabama General Store began to show a profit on their books. The store became famous for its fresh produce and excellent meat selection. People began coming from a radius of over fifty miles to shop at this obscure, family-owned market.

Nelson continued to give the groceries to the Indian population that they needed to survive, always asking them to sign their names with an "X." He kept a special account book just for those who lived on the reservation and as the Depression marched on, the pages were filled with thousands of dollars of indebtedness.

When World War II broke out, the Indians no longer came to the Alabama General Store as often because times had changed and they were now able to make a living. Many of their sons, the little boys whom Nelson had fed, now fought and died in service to their country. At the end of World War II, Nelson was diagnosed with diabetes and he knew his work on Earth was nearly done. One evening, he had his wife, Mary, call the Indian chief to their small home. Nelson held the ledger book in his wrinkled hands that detailed the accounts of the thousands and thousands of dollars owned to him by the Indian nation.

Nelson asked the Indian chief to follow him to their backyard where Nelson's son, Don, had prepared a roaring fire. Nelson, his wife Mary, their three children, and the Indian chief watched the ledger book and the thousands of dollars of indebtedness disappear and burn into oblivion. Nelson had his miracle. It began the first day he gave what he could not afford to give. The miracle of abundant life is what God *always* provides for givers.

Prayer for Life

"Dear Jesus, I love You so much and I thank You that You always provide for givers. Thank You for calming the storms in my life and I ask that You will do the greater miracles through me. In Your powerful name I pray, Amen."

Declaration for Life

"I declare that it is impossible to out-give God. I declare that I will be a giver regardless of the economy or of the health of my bank accounts. I declare that I will keep my eyes fixed on Jesus during every storm in life. I declare that my life will partner with the power of Heaven to do greater works during my time on Earth."

Scripture for Life

"Give and it will be given to you. They will pour into your lap a good measure—pressed down, shaken together, and running over. For by your standard of measure it will be measured to you in return" (Luke 6:38).

Words of Life

"You face your greatest opposition when you are closest to your biggest miracle." — *T. D. Jakes*

CHAPTER 11

Living for Legacy

THIS is the chapter you have been waiting for ... this chapter holds the truth that needs to soak deeply into your soul. Although the story of the person whose life this chapter is highlighting won't be revealed until the end, I know when you discover who it is, you will be forever changed.

One of the most compelling and valuable aspects of abundant life is that you don't die the day you stop breathing.

I am not referencing your entrance into Heaven, although I can guarantee you that Heaven is indeed a real place and once you arrive there, Earth will no longer hold any power over your heart and mind. The legacy you have the potential to leave as you exit this tangible world is a generous slice of the abundance Jesus has given to you this side of Heaven. You have the power and influence to impact people on Earth beyond your death. The choices you are making today wield a massive influence on your vibrant call to impact people on Earth when you have changed your address to Heaven. Live in such a grand and healthy manner that your legacy outlasts that dash on your tombstone.

With No One's Regret

Matthew is our oldest child and the firstborn of the five creative, passionate, enthusiastic young adults whose last name just happens to be McLeod. He has possessed a type A personality since the day he exited my womb in January of 1981. Matt was an athlete, scholar, and leader while in high school and college. He chose the girl of my dreams and is an amazing father to three of the brightest and most beautiful grandbabies known to mankind. He is a young adult pastor and high school basketball coach in the great state of Texas. In his career of coaching varsity boys' basketball for only six years, he has been named "Texas Basketball Coach of the Year" twice in the private school division. This young man, who holds a special place in my heart, has had extraordinary success both on and off the court.

Matt has chosen a particular Scripture to hang above his office door. He sees this same Scripture every time he walks out of his office into a meeting, onto the ball court, into a time of confrontation with parents or administrators, into chapel, or into the community. This Scripture serves to remind Matt the importance of living for legacy:

"He was thirty-two years old when he became king,
and he reigned in Jerusalem eight years; and he
departed with no one's regret, and they buried him in
the city of David, but not in the tombs of the kings"
(2 Chronicles 21:20).

It is most likely you have never heard of the king this Scripture is referencing because *"he departed with no one's regret."* This king refused, by the everyday choices he made, to leave a lasting legacy. No one missed this man when he was gone, even though he was crowned king of one of the largest kingdoms at his time in history. His name was King Jehoram and he willfully chose to die without making any earthly impact beyond his years of breathing oxygen. No one remembers what he did, who trusted him, what he cherished, and or what he said. It's one thing to die and it's quite another thing altogether to die without making an impact. We will all die someday—no one can change that fact. However, we can all choose how we will be remembered after we die. It is up to you ... no one else but you. God wants you to be remembered with significance and with impact, but He has given you the freedom of choice in your everyday matters. How you choose to live will create your legacy and whether or not you will depart with anyone's regret.

King Jehoram was forty years old when he died which,

admittedly, is young by today's standards. He had been king for eight years, which is the same as a two-term United States president. He had the same opportunity to leave a lasting and memorable legacy as did Ronald Reagan, George Washington, and Thomas Jefferson. However, there were no mourners at King Jehoram's funeral. No one cried when he died or wasted a tissue over his mid-life death. Most of the people were muttering things under their breath like, "Good riddance!"

King Jehoram was buried, but not with the kings. There was no state funeral for this man and no flags flying at half-staff. There was no honor attached to his sordid name, so rotten was the life he had chosen to live.

It was the highest honor of one's life at this time in history to be buried in the tombs of the kings and King Jehoram had been given the extraordinary chance to have that opportunity. He could have been remembered for greatness and for goodness. He could have been remembered for his impeccable leadership skills and for wisdom and kindness. But he refused all of that because self got in the way of greatness and of legacy.

David was the first person to be buried in the tombs of the kings and David was far from perfect. But he left a legacy because of his heart—he was the man after God's own heart and what a rich legacy that is! David also left the legacy of leadership and of worship. From King David we learn that one does not have to live a perfect and spotless life in order to leave a lasting legacy. One just needs to chase after God in spite of imperfections.

King Jehoram lived like Earth was all there was to life. In spite of the title "king," Jehoram undistinguished himself and chose not to live like a king, but like a madman. He had the opportunity for moral and historical greatness as king, but he threw it all away because of his emotional outrage and instability. This man identified by the title King Jehoram refused to honor God or obey God in his daily life decisions.

Many of the richest legacies known to mankind have been left by the poorest of people; some of the most significant legacies have been crafted and designed by the most insignificant of people on Earth. Some of the longest lasting legacies have been left by the youngest of people to die.

"The memory of the righteous is blessed, but the name of the wicked will rot" (Proverbs 10:7).

In my Bible, right beside this particular verse, I have written these two significant words, "That's me!"

How you choose to live your life matters; it counts today and it counts after your feet have left the confines of an earthly and mortal existence. Part of your ability to tap into an abundant life, that which is life indeed, is choosing to live in such a significant manner that people actually regret it when you die. If you choose to live well today and tomorrow and in all the tomorrows yet to come, the people who know you will mourn your passing. Your acquaintances will wish they had known you better and your friends will regret they did not spend enough time in your presence. Whether a well-known celebrity or an insignificant person with an unknown address, when you live for legacy you will be remembered as one who lived with gusto and honor and chose to be a significant person in the Kingdom of God.

All of the things you may think help to leave a significant legacy may not actually be enormously vital to leaving a resounding impact on history. Neither prominence, wealth, an elected office, platform, good looks, nor an Ivy League education guarantee your life will make ripples on the glorious pond of life. The echo your life has the power to make may lie in two simple, but resounding, choices.

To be Kind

Joy was our first daughter born after the adventure and activity of three boys in a row. The people at our North Carolina church were thrilled with the softness and dainty delight of buying pink dresses, lacy socks, and Nellie Olson hair bows for the newest member of the McLeod family. We had so many girlie dresses given to us that she did not wear the same dress to church for nearly sixteen months. It was ridiculous and I loved every single minute of it.

When Joy was old enough to understand how the people at church were absolutely doting over her, I knew I had to begin to train her in some basic relationship skills before they created a spoiled, self-centered, obnoxious piece of femininity. When she reached two years old, every Sunday on the way home from church, our conversation was one of training and of redirecting her impressionable heart.

"Joy-Belle," I would say from the front seat of the twelve-passenger Dodge Ram van, "Is it more important to be pretty or to be kind?"

She would take her pacifier out of her rosebud mouth, look at my reflection in the rearview mirror, and say, "To be kind, Mama, to be kind."

Kindness is an incomparable attribute that will enable you to leave a defining mark on the world in which you live. Kindness is more valuable than gold, more significant than worldwide fame, and more vital than a respected education. There is a woman in the Bible who was known for leaving this type of legacy. Her story is told in Proverbs 31.

"She opens her mouth in wisdom and the teaching of kindness is on her tongue" (Proverbs 31:26).

The word *teaching* in this valuable and challenging verse is sometimes translated as law, but the most accurate description of this Hebrew word is found in a cluster of words defined as *custom, habit, or manner.* Kindness was the ruling authority of this singular and wise woman's mouth. Her legacy reverberates through every decade of Christendom. This woman, whom the

Bible holds up as the one woman of distinctive emulation, was always careful to speak, encourage, correct, instruct, and advise with the words and the attitude of simple kindness.

Is kindness the ruling authority of your tongue? Kindness should be in charge of every word, every voice inflection, every attitude, and every tone that comes out of your mouth. As believers who desire to leave a long-lasting legacy and to live a life of genuine abundance, we must choose kindness over anger, opinion, and pride. It is not enough just to be kind to those who are kind to you, but the kindness of your life should thrive in all types of emotional and relational climates. Developing the habit of kind thoughts that are followed by kind words and kind deeds is one of the most significant choices you can make if you desire to leave a legacy that lives beyond your dash.

What Seed Have You Planted?

All fruit begins with a simple seed; there will be no fruit if there is no seed. Kindness is a fruit of the Holy Spirit and for this fruit to flourish in your life you must sweetly and humbly plant the seed of kindness in your life with the healthy and productive presence of the Holy Spirit. The character of the fruit produced is always determined by the character of the seed that has been planted. Fruit always has the DNA of the seed embedded inside of it. If your desire is to leave a legacy of simple yet resilient kindness, then you must choose to plant seeds of kindness because fruit always produces after its own kind. An orange farmer never worries that he might be producing a harvest of grapes because he knows exactly what seeds have been planted in his orchards.

You choose to either plant seeds of self or seeds of the Holy Spirit. In order to plant the luscious, vibrant, and delicious crop of the Holy Spirit, you must hang out with the Holy Spirit. If you refuse to spend time in the presence of the Holy Spirit, listening to His voice and learning from Him, you will allow the world's ideas, convictions, and opinions to become part of the fiber and produce of your life. When you die to self, and plant the powerful seed of the Holy Spirit in your life and in your heart, then it is a guarantee that the fruit of your life will be delicious! The juice of Heaven's abundance will be running down your chin and you will have more than enough to share with the world around you.

"What is desirable in a man is his kindness ..."
(Proverbs 19:22).

The anecdote for loneliness is kindness because people love to develop long-lasting relationships with truly kind people. When kindness is your fruit of choice, you will have a bevy of friends simply because you are such a pleasurable experience for them. People will want multiple servings of you when the habit of kindness is on your tongue and you will taste just delicious to the world around you.

Superlatives

The day before I began my first year of high school, my mother called me into our living room for a heart-to-heart conversation. These were the words she spoke to me that memorable day and they have echoed into my life although over four decades have passed:

"Carol, you are about to begin one of the most important seasons of your life. The memories you create and the friendships you make over the next four years will most likely shape your life in ways that nothing else will. Carol, you will not be the most popular girl in the freshman class. You will not be the most musical, the smartest, the most athletic, or the prettiest. But what you can be is the kindest. Make it your number one priority to be the kindest girl in your entire class."

The reason my mother made that life-altering speech to me that day was because her mother had said the exact same words to her the day before she commenced her high school experience. And, as you have probably guessed, I had the exact same conversation with all five of my smart, good-looking, musical, athletic children the day before they began high school.

Kindness = Gentleness

"But the fruit of the Spirit is love, joy, peace,
patience, kindness, goodness, faithfulness, gentleness,
self-control; against such things there is no law"
(Galatians 5:22-23).

As you begin to choose to taste like the fruit of kindness, you will soon discover that kindness is always gentle and that gentleness is always kind. It is impossible to have one without the other because kindness is never abrasive, assertive, or rough. Both kindness and gentleness communicate the life skill of being adaptable to other's needs with love leading the way. Neither kindness nor gentleness is a characteristic our culture values or promotes. Our culture has deceived us into believing we should demand our own way, walk over people to get to the top, and certainly never allow anyone to push us out of the way. The mentality and emotional strategy that is birthed from the culture in which we live demands we say everything we think, feel, and believe.

Kindness, which has always been the strategy of God in a cruel and unkind world, talks like this,

"How can I serve you?"

"How can I make your life easier?"

"Is there anything I can do for you?"

When God requires His children to be kind, it is much more than just a suggestion.

"He has told you, O man, what is good; and what
does the Lord require of you but to do justice, to
love kindness, and to walk humbly with your God?"
(Micah 6:8).

God is sitting you down and speaking into your life today. He is reminding you that of all of the characteristics, gifts, talents, and abilities you may possess, it is kindness that is of the utmost importance to Him.

"Or do you think lightly of the riches of His
kindness and tolerance and patience, not knowing
that the kindness of God leads you to repentance?"
(Romans 2:4).

What an incredible verse! If God's kindness leads sinners to repentance ... guess what? The kindness you exhibit to difficult and fractious people just may make a difference in their lives as well. When you choose to be identified with the fruit of the Spirit known as simple kindness, you have the potential to change someone else's life. Your delicious fruit, that comes from the DNA of God, may lead someone to Jesus and help undo the chains of sin. Kindness is a powerful piece of fruit.

The Legacy of Courage

Peter and John had spent three years of their lives in the presence of Jesus Christ. They were among the men who had developed the very closest of relationships with the Man who healed the sick, raised the dead, and walked on water. They had spent time with Jesus snoring, laughing, listening, and learning. These two extraordinary men, after Jesus had risen from the dead and then ascended to Heaven, left a legacy that is unparalleled in human history.

Peter and John were speaking to the people recounted in Acts 4, and telling them about Jesus and His Resurrection from the dead. On one day alone, over 5,000 people believed in the truth of the Gospel of Jesus Christ. The religious leaders of the day were greatly disturbed over the testimony and preaching of Peter and John and put them in jail overnight.

When Peter and John were released from jail the next day, the religious authority figures asked them, "By what power, or in what name, have you done this?"

Then Peter, filled with the Holy Spirit, gave them a powerful answer that echoes through the centuries.

"And there is salvation in no one else; for there is no other name under heaven that has been given among men by which we must be saved" (Acts 4:12).

The Holy Spirit can give you the same confidence and boldness that was given to Peter that day. This courage is a courage that is impossible to stir up, pretend, or imitate. The courage and boldness that Peter exhibited can only be given to you by the Holy Spirit. This is a boldness that rulers will not be able to intimidate, days spent in jail will not discourage, and the crowds of our culture will never be able to silence. When the Holy Spirit endows a believer with the power of Heaven, there is no force on Earth that can silence the voice or the impact of this life.

The desire to be a bold and powerful witness at this time in history is, in reality, the only legacy that is worthy of our focus. The courage to speak out for the gospel, without fear of offending people, is the courage that should top every prayer list of every determined believer.

"God! Give me the courage of Peter and John!"

Having Been With Jesus

"Now as they observed the confidence of Peter and John and understood that they were uneducated

and untrained men, they were amazed, and began to
recognize themas having been with Jesus." (Acts 4:13).

In reading this Scripture that follows the story of preaching, imprisonment, and boldness, the first question I am confronted with is, "Who is *they*"?

Who is the *they* who observed the confidence of Peter and John and were amazed, and at last realized these men had been with Jesus? The *they* are the same authority figures who had thrown them into jail and who had been disturbed by what Peter and John had been talking about.

Education has nothing to do with boldness and neither does training. It is purely *"having been with Jesus"* that gives even modern-day disciples all of the confidence they need to confront difficult and intimidating situations and people. The boldness that was observed in Peter and John by the leading religious figures of the day was a Spirit-inspired courage and a Heaven-birthed confidence that enabled Peter and John to speak forthrightly in spite of any danger or threat.

The religious leaders commanded Peter and John not to speak or teach at all in the name of Jesus. And yet Peter and John, because of having been with Jesus and having been filled with the Holy Spirit, knew there was no power on Earth that could keep them quiet. Peter and John refused to allow any government of man to press the mute button on their powerful tongues.

"But Peter and John answered and said to them,
'Whether it is right in the sight of God to give heed
to you rather than to God, you be the judge; for we
cannot stop speaking about what we have seen and
heard'" (Acts 4:19-20).

Is that your testimony as well? Are you unable to stop speaking about what you have seen and heard? There are many intimidating issues and people who may try to muzzle your testimony. Part of your ability to tap into a life so abundant that you are unable to measure its wealth is found in your confrontation of mindsets, cultures, and religion just like Peter and John did.

Life this side of Heaven is much too short and if you desire to live beyond the length of your life then you will speak up with confidence. You will tell others about your Savior ... but may I just encourage you to be kind first? Kindness will earn you the right to speak forth with boldness.

Some Shakin'!

If you have not read one Scripture reference in this entire book, I dare you to read the verses that follow. You cannot afford to skip over or underestimate the power of the prayer that is contained in these verses.

> *"And now, Lord, take note of their threats, and grant that Your bond-servants may speak Your word with all confidence, while You extend Your hand to heal, and signs and wonders take place through the name of Your holy servant Jesus." And when they had prayed, the place where they had gathered together was shaken, and they were all filled with the Holy Spirit and began to speak the word of God with boldness.* (Acts 4:29-31)

Are you brave enough to pray the prayer that was prayed by John and Peter nearly 2,000 years ago? Are you bold enough to open up your life for the power of the Holy Spirit to fill your mouth and your heart? If you are ... get ready for some shakin'! Ask God to give you every kind of boldness that He has in the resources of Heaven.

Ask God for marketplace boldness ...

Ask God for family boldness ...

Ask God for boldness with your neighbors and in restaurants ...

Ask God for boldness at the gym and at the nail salon ...

Ask God for boldness in the doctor's office and at the mall!

The boldness that God desires to bequeath to you as part of your abundant life will include boldness and an unreservedness in your speech with others. You can remain kind and gentle and yet still share the Word of God without reserve. Remind yourself not to talk in circles or become defensive, but just give the straight-up truth with cheerful courage and fearless confidence.

The word *boldness* in the Greek is translated as this: "the deportment by which one becomes conspicuous." During my decades of abundant living and more life than I deserve on planet Earth, the cry of my heart is that I would become conspicuous for Jesus. There is no other reason to live than to be a bold, kind, powerful witness of the Gospel of Jesus Christ at this time in history. No other reason at all!

Dead Bones

When Elijah, the great prophet of the Old Testament was dying, he asked his young protégé, Elisha, what he desired from him. Elisha boldly asked for a double portion of Elijah's powerful anointing. Elisha died while having performed exactly one less than double the amount of miracles his predecessor, Elijah, had performed. Elisha nearly got what he had asked for; he had received just one less than twice as much.

Elisha died, and they buried him. Now the bands of the Moabites would invade the land in the spring of the year. As they were burying a man, behold, they saw a marauding band; and they cast the man into the grave of Elisha. And when the man touched the bones of Elisha he revived and stood up on his feet. (2 Kings 13:20-21)

This miracle, of bringing a man back to life although Elisha was dead, completed the double anointing Elisha had requested on his life. With this final impact of the life of Elisha, he completed exactly twice as many miracles as did Elijah.

Elisha's bones were some mighty powerful dead bones! There was life indeed in the dead bones of Elisha. There was abundant life in the dead bones of Elisha. There was absolutely nothing ordinary about the dead bones of Elisha. There was legacy in the dead bones of the prophet Elisha.

Will your bones be dead-dead bones? Or will your dead bones continue to give life even after you have left the constraints of planet Earth? Elisha lived on although he had ceased to breathe; miracles continued on beyond the life of Elisha because of his absolute boldness in prayer.

- When you die, will your life continue to cause others to live?
- Will you leave a legacy of courage and kindness?
- Will you be remembered for something so miraculous and so powerful that you live beyond yourself?

No More Ordinary!

I have waited until the end of this, the final chapter, to tell you the stirring story of the person whose life has made a profound difference at this our moment in history. I believe you actually know this person very well. In fact ... you eat with this person at every meal and actually think like this incredible person. You dress like this person and understand this person better than anyone else on the face of planet Earth at this time in history.

You are the hero of the faith whose story concludes this book on abundant life.

Will your life be an inspiration to others?
Only you can determine that.

Will someone count you as their hero or heroine of the faith?
Only you can determine that.

Are you willing to make hard choices?
Only you can determine that.

Are you willing to be kind and to be courageous?
Only you can determine that.

Are you willing to serve the Kingdom of God in spite of insurmountable odds?
Only you can determine that.

Are you willing to choose the joy of His presence when your world is falling apart?
Only you can determine that.

Are you willing to forgive someone who simply doesn't deserve it?
Only you can determine that.

Will you give generously and unselfishly to others when you can't afford it?
Only you can determine that.

You choose the end of your story. You choose whether or not to live a life so abundant that the angels gasp. You choose whether or not to tap into the *life indeed* that has been offered to you. You choose whether or not to access the life Jesus died for. You choose whether to settle into a merely ordinary existence, or to partner with God in a life that declares for the world to hear, "No More Ordinary! I will live the life for which I was created!" You choose.

Prayer for Life

"Dear Jesus, I love You so much. I pray that Your story will be boldly, kindly, and triumphantly lived out through my life. I pray that I will leave a legacy that has been strategically determined by Your promise of abundant life. In Your life-giving name I pray, Amen."

Declaration for Life

"I declare that I will leave a legacy of hope and joy. I declare that my bones will not be dead-dead, but they will be lively, miraculous bones. I declare that even when I am no longer on planet Earth, the miracles Jesus did through me and the impact of my existence will echo through the hallways of history. I declare that my life will be more than ordinary and that I will live the life for which I was made!

Scripture for Life

"And now, Lord, take note of their threats, and grant that Your bond-servants may speak Your word with all confidence, while You extend Your hand to heal, and signs and wonders take place through the name of Your holy servant Jesus." And when they had prayed, the place where they had gathered together was shaken, and they were all filled with the Holy Spirit and began to speak the word of God with boldness. (Acts 4:29-31)

Words of Life

"Our days are numbered. One of the primary goals in our lives should be to prepare for our last day. The legacy we leave is not just in our possessions, but in the quality of our lives. What preparations should we be making now? The greatest waste in all of our Earth, which cannot be recycled or reclaimed, is our waste of the time that God has given us each day." — *Billy Graham*

Acknowledgements

Oh my ... how grateful I am for the fingerprints and voices of so many significant people who have loved me ... prayed for me ... and supported me during the journey of *No More Ordinary!*

Craig ... You have made my life so much more than ordinary. Ours is an extraordinary love for which I am grateful every day of my life.

Matthew and Emily ... you model what this book is all about. Your story is being written by the pen of the Holy Spirit and will impact the generations to come. I believe in you and I love you both.

Christopher and Liz ... your hearts and kindness are extraordinary gifts to this family and to me personally. What is being created by your lives is nothing short of glorious! I believe in you and I love you both.

Jordan and Allie ... every day I spend with you is a delight and a joy! Never stop dreaming or becoming all that God intended for you to be! I believe in you and I love you both.

Joy ... When you were a little girl, you gave me a dish that said, "A daughter is a little girl who grows up to be your friend." That gift was prophetic, wasn't it?! I love being your mom, working with you in ministry and being your friend! I believe in you and I love you.

Joni ... You are learning how to use your wings and they are beautiful and strong. I pray that your wings will take you fully and joyfully into God's destiny for your life! You are always ... always ... in my heart. I believe in you and I love you.

Olivia, Ian, Wesley, Amelia and Boyce ... the next generation of the clan McLeod! I love the sparkle in your eyes ... the giggle in your hearts ... and your little arms around my neck. Always remember that there is nothing more important in life than simply loving Jesus.

Mom and Leo ... Your strength, support and prayers are gifts that are priceless to me in this season of my life. I ache to be with you every day. Take care of one another! Thank you for being extraordinary people whom this family looks up to with great respect and honor.

Nanny ... Thank you for sweeping my floors, cooking my meals and praying while I am working. You are loved and we are honored to have you with us in this season.

Stevie ... my brother and my friend. You are living so well! I am proud to say that I am your big sister. Know that I am always cheering and praying for you. Your faith is amazing and calls me higher.

King David ... Uncle Moe ... Your prayers and support are foundational cornerstones in my life and ministry. When we get to heaven ... you will get the credit!! Who knew that an award-winning football coach would find so much joy in partnering with a women's ministry?!! God knew ...

Dad ... although you are now in heaven ... everything that I am today is because God gave you to me as my father. You will always be a general of the faith and a man of great wisdom and courage. I know that now you are part of my cloud of witnesses cheering loudly as I make my mark on this moment in history! Tell Jesus how much I love Him!!

Monica, Angel, Jamie and Joy ... my comrades in ministry ... my co-workers ... my prayer warriors ... my dearest friends. How I love your hearts ... your minds ... your passion and your genuine enthusiasm for all things JOY! Let's keep dreaming Godsized dreams and changing this world together!!

Janie, Loren, Jenna, Ashley and Avery ... you are truly family to us. Thank you for making us laugh and for giving us opportunities to celebrate family, friendship and the life we have been given!

Kelly, Kerri and Sarah ... You will always be daughters of my heart and the lives upon which this ministry was built. Raise your families well ... teach them to read their Bibles ... and to serve Christ passionately! You are modeling by your lives that it really does pay to serve Jesus!

John Mason ... "Thank You" does not seem like enough and it will never be enough. You are one amazing man! Your joy is contagious ... your heart is massive ... and your wisdom is boggling. Just keep being who you were created to be! Is your literary agent supposed to be one of your dearest friends?! Is that possible?!

Julie and Scott Spiewak ... **FreshImpact PR** ... Heaven applauded the day that you walked into my life. I am humbled to serve God with you by my side. Thanks for being genuine and godly. I pray that God blesses you and your girls enormously because of your labor love in the Kingdom.

Chris and the team at LightQuest ... I love shaking and earth with you! It is no small thing to work with people who are ferocious in their approach. You embody both!

Peggy and Lloyd Hildebrand and the Bridge-Logos family ... The message of your lives is a lighthouse in the challenging world of the publishing industry. Thanks for believing in me and in the message of this book. I am praying for you as you serve God!

Carolyn Hogan, Shannon Maitre, Lynn Fields, Dawn Frink, Marilyn Frebersyser, Debbie Edwards, Susie Hilchey, Kim Pickard-Dudley, Lisa Keller, Melissa Schutrum ... Lifetime girlfriends. Prayer warriors. Giggle inducers. Secret keepers. Dream believers. Cheerleaders. Wisdom givers. Each one of you is a valuable treasure. I am richer for having known you!

And most importantly ... the highest praise of my heart goes to Jesus ... my first Love and dearest Friend. Without You ... nothing is possible. With you ... all things are possible!!

If you are interested in having Carol McLeod speak at your conference or Women's Retreat, please contact us:

Just Joy! Ministries
PO Box 1294
Orchard Park, NY 14127

(by phone) 855-569-5433
(by email) info@justjoyministries.com
For more information, visit our website at
www.JustJoyMinistries.com

**Life Changing, Word Driven Books & Teachings
by Carol McLeod**

Holy Estrogen	Defiant Joy
Rooms of a Woman's Heart	Never, Never, Never Give Up
More Than Happy Ever	After Life Indeed
Who Do You Think You Are	Miracle of Motherhood
Pure Gold	Joy in All Seasons
Hope Scriptures	Healing Scriptures
Joy 150X	

YouVersion

21 Days to Beat Depression
Jolt of Joy
Joy to YOUR World
Holy Emotions
For the Joy Set Before Him

Check our website to
see the station information
for your town!
Podcasts also available on
the website.

All books and CD/DVD teachings are available
on the Just Joy! website
www.JustJoyMinistries.com